The Historic
COUNTRY HOUSES
of Leicestershire and Rutland

Leonard Cantor

KAIROS PRESS

Newtown Linford

Leicester

1998

ISBN 1-871344-18-2

First Edition, 1998

Design and Layout by Robin Stevenson, Kairos Press
Body text in Century Schoolbook BT 10.5pt
Imagesetting by Double Vision, Leicester
Printed in Great Britain by Norwood Press, Anstey, Leics.

Front Cover: Burley-on-the-Hill, Rutland

Back Cover, left to right: Coleorton Hall, Market Bosworth Hall, Belvoir Castle,
Quenby Hall, Hambleton Old Hall

KAIROS PRESS
552 Bradgate Road,
Newtown Linford
Leicester LE6 0HB
Great Britain.

Contents

List of Figures *4*

Acknowledgements *5*

Preface *6*

*Part 1: The History of the Country Houses
of Leicestershire and Rutland* *7*

*Part 2: Gazetteer
Leicestershire* *32*

Rutland *73*

Glossary of Architectural Terms *81*

Visiting and Looking at our Country Houses *82*

Bibliography and References *83*

Index *84*

List of Figures

1.	The ruins of Ashby Castle	8
2.	Ashby Castle, the Hastings Tower	8
3.	The ruins of Kirby Muxloe Castle	9
4.	An engraving of Bradgate House, about 1700	10
5.	The ruins of Bradgate House	10
6.	The east wing of Stapleford Park	11
7.	The ruins of Cavendish House, Abbey Park, Leicester	12
8.	A Plan of the site of Kirby Bellars Hall	13
9.	The pattern of diapers in brick buildings	14
10.	Market Bosworth Hall	14
11.	Staunton Harold Hall	14
12.	Belvoir Castle	15
13.	Burley-on-the-Hill	15
14.	Ragdale Old Hall, demolished in 1958	16
15.	The ruins of Exton Old Hall, burnt down in 1810	17
16.	A drawing of Martinsthorpe Hall, Rutland	17
17.	Stanford Hall	18
18.	Withcote Hall	19
19.	Architural styles, 1485 – 1910	18-19
20.	Belgrave Hall, Leicester	20
21.	Garendon Hall, Loughborough, built in the 1730s	20
22.	The Temple of Venus in Garendon Park	21
23.	Gopsall Hall, built between 1747 and 1749	21
24.	Gumley Hall, built in 1764 and demolished in 1964	22
25.	Donington Hall, the porch on the main front	23
26.	Buckminster Park, demolished in 1952	23
27.	The south front of Quorn House	24
28.	The early seventeenth-century Beaumanor Hall	25
29.	Belvoir Castle in the eighteenth century	25
30.	Donington Hall in the eighteenth century	25
31.	A Plan of Cotes Hall, near Loughborough	28
32.	Edmondthorpe Hall before it burned down in 1942.	28
33.	Danets Hall, Leicester, demolished in 1861	28
34.	Tickencote Hall, Rutland, demolished in the 1950s	28
35.	Papillon Hall, near Lubenham, demolished in 1950	29
36.	Normanton Hall, Rutland, pulled down in 1926	29
37.	Burleigh Hall, Loughborough, demolished in 1961	29
38.	Ashby Folville Manor	32
39.	Baggrave Hall, the west front	33
40.	Barkby Hall, the entrance front	34
41.	Beaumanor Park, the entrance front	34
42.	Belgrave Hall, Leicester, the garden front	35
43.	Belvoir Castle	36
44.	Braunstone Hall	37
45.	Brooksby Hall	38
46.	Carlton Curlieu Hall	39
47.	Cold Overton Hall, garden front	39
48.	Cold Overton Hall, the porch	40
49.	Coleorton Hall	41
50.	Donington Hall	42
51.	Gaddesby Hall, the south-west front	43
52.	Goadby Marwood Hall, the south front	44
53.	Grace Dieu Manor	45
54.	Husbands Bosworth Hall	46
55.	Ingarsby Old Hall	46
56.	Keythorpe Hall	47
57.	Langton Hall	48
58.	Launde Abbey	49
59.	Lockington Hall, the entrance front	50
60.	Lockington Hall, the garden front	50
61.	Lowesby Hall, the entrance front	51
62.	Lowesby Hall, the garden front	51
63.	Market Bosworth Hall, the west front	52
64.	Nevill Holt Hall	53
65.	Nevill Holt Hall, the fifteenth-century bay window	54
66.	Noseley Hall	55
67.	Osbaston Hall, the east range	55
68.	Osbaston Hall, the south entrance front	56
69.	Peatling Parva Hall, the garden front	56
70.	Prestwold Hall, the garden front	57
71.	Quenby Hall, the west entrance front	58
72.	Quorn Hall, the south front	59
73.	Quorn House, the west front	60
74.	Rothley Hall, the entrance front	61
75.	Scraptoft Hall, the west front	62
76.	Scraptoft Hall, the eighteenth-century gates	62
77.	Shenton Hall, the seventeenth-century gatehouse	63
78.	Skeffington Hall	63
79.	Stanford Hall	64
80.	Stapleford Park	66
81.	Staunton Harold Hall and chapel	67
82.	Stretton Hall	68
83.	Swithland Hall, the garden front	69
84.	Whatton House, the entrance front	70
85.	Whatton House, the garden front	70
86.	Wistow Hall, the entrance front	71
87.	Withcote Hall, the garden front	72
88.	Ayston Hall	73
89.	Burley-on-the-Hill, the south front	74
90.	Burley-on-the-Hill, the north front and colonnade	74
91.	Clipsham Hall, the east front	75
92.	Exton Hall, the west front	75
93.	Hambledon Hall, the south front	76
94.	Hambledon Old Hall, the entrance front	77
95.	Langham Old Hall, the south front	77
96.	Lyndon Hall, the east front	78
97.	North Luffenham Hall, the entrance front	78
98.	North Luffenham Hall, the north front	79
99.	South Luffenham Hall, the garden front	79
100.	Tolethorpe Hall, the north front	80

Acknowledgements

A number of people have helped me to write this book and I wish to express my thanks to them: to Tony Squires for reading the draft text and making helpful suggestions; to Dr Christopher Brook and his colleagues of the Leicestershire County Council Buildings Conservation Team for allowing me to use their architectural notes and for supplying me with photographs; to the staff of the Leicestershire Record Office for their help and for granting me permission to reproduce some items in their care; to Robert F. Hartley, Curator of Market Harborough Museum, for allowing me to use two of his excellent drawings; to Simon Jones, Planning Officer, Rutland Council Offices, for providing me with architectural notes and photographs of country houses in Rutland; to Bryan Waites for allowing me to draw upon his extensive knowledge of Rutland and to use photographs in his book, "A Celebration of Rutland"; to the Head of Department and staff of the Education Department, Loughborough University, for giving me free run of their reprographic facilities; to Robin Stevenson of Kairos Press for his support, enthusiasm and technological expertise; and last but not least to the owners of country houses who, virtually without exception, received me kindly and allowed me to photograph their historic homes.

Illustration Credits

I wish to thank the following for permission to use their copyright photographs and drawings:

Robert F. Hartley: Figures 8 and 31
The Leicestershire Record Office: Figures 14, 21, 23, 24, 26, 32, 35, 56, 78
Bryan Waites: Figures 16, 33, 36
Department of Planning and Transportation, Peter Foss: Drawing on page 6, from *The History of Market Bosworth* (1983)

Leicestershire County Council: Figures 46, 51, 52, 54, 61, 62, 64, 65, 66, 69, 77
Major J. Gillies Shields: Figure 30
Planning Office, Rutland Council Offices: Figures 88, 92, 95, 97, 98
All other illustrations are by the author

A Note on Sources

Throughout the book I have drawn extensively for architectural details on Nikolaus Pevsner, *The Buildings of Leicestershire and Rutland*, Second Edition, Revised by Elizabeth Williamson with Geoffrey K. Brandwood, Penguin Books, 1984. For Leicestershire buildings, I have also made considerable use of the detailed architectural accounts made available to me by the Leicestershire Department of Planning and Transportation at County Hall. For Leicestershire family histories, I have used Heather E. Broughton, *Family and Estate Records in the Leicestershire Record Office*, Leicestershire Museums, Arts and Record Service, 1991. For Rutland buildings, I have used the architectural notes in the Council Offices in Oakham and for Rutland families, Bryan Waites (Ed.), *Who Was Who in Rutland*, Rutland Record, No.8, 1988. Where particular sources are used for individual houses, specific reference is made to them.

Preface

We are very fortunate indeed in our inheritance of country houses many of which, in Leicestershire and Rutland as throughout England, are of considerable historical, architectural and artistic interest. Their owners built, and in many cases rebuilt, them over a period of almost 500 years, set them in beautiful parkland and filled them with fine furniture and works of art. Although many have come and gone over the centuries, it is only in the last 100 years that, for reasons spelled out in the book, we have lost large numbers of them. Happily, the haemorrhaging stopped in the 1970s and as I have attempted to show we still have many fine houses in the two counties, a substantial proportion of which remain in private hands. Others have been sold by their former owners to become hotels, hospitals, educational establishments and the like, or divided into separate units. At the very least this has ensured the survival of the houses and their general well-being. In this book I have, where possible, given a brief account of the families who built them and lived in them. I have also concentrated on their architectural features, partly because these are most easily seen and partly because that is where my main interests lie. Finally, while I have tried to be comprehensive in my coverage of our historic country houses, doubtless I have inadvertently omitted some and for that I apologise.

Leonard Cantor
September 1998

Cartouche in the south front pediment at Market Bosworth Hall.

PART 1

The History of the Country Houses of Leicestershire and Rutland

What is an historic Country House?

At first sight, the definition of "an historic Country House" may seem fairly straightforward. In practice, however, it is more complex and may be determined by such criteria as the age and size of the house, its architectural interest or lack of it, the history of the families who have lived in it, and the extent of the parkland which surrounds it. For the purposes of this book, I have- albeit with a good degree of flexibility- adopted the criteria followed by Littlejohn in his book on English country houses[1]: namely, a large private residence which has served as a family home for some generations; a substantial house which frequently contains fine furniture and works of art; and one which is, or has been, set in its own parkland and acted as the focal point for the local countryside In the great majority of cases, particularly those houses which have existed for centuries, they have been added to and altered so that they bear the stamp of several different architectural styles. By these criteria, though we have lost many historic country houses, England as a whole still contains up to 2,000 of them, about two-thirds of which are still in private hands and about one-fifth open to public view for at least part of the year.[2] As we shall see, Leicestershire and Rutland have their fair share of these houses which make so distinctive a contribution to the English countryside and to our architectural and artistic heritage.

Medieval Beginnings

The first true English country houses date from the reign of Henry VII, 1485 to 1509, following the troubled times of the Wars of the Roses, which lasted from the mid-1450s to his accession to the throne following his victory at the Battle of Bosworth. During earlier centuries there were a number of manor houses built in the two counties. Often surrounded by moats, they included *Donington-le-Heath*, *Appleby Magna* and *Ashby-de-la-Zouch*. In the case of the latter two, they were replaced by later buildings. However, these buildings met few of the criteria listed above for country houses and were essentially relatively modest homes for the lords of the manor, in or near their villages.

The immediate ancestor to the country house was the fortified house, of which there are two fine examples in Leicestershire, both known as "castles" in deference to their medieval predecessors, namely Ashby-de-la-Zouch Castle and Kirby Muxloe Castle. As Hoskins puts it, "Neither Ashby nor Kirby is a true castle, but a strongly fortified dwelling-house built....by a powerful feudal lord who had good reason to barricade himself in".[3] The powerful lord in question was William, Lord Hastings, Lord Chaberlain and close associate of the reigning king,

the Civil War was held by the King and besieged by the Roundheads for 15 months before it was surrendered in February 1646. In 1648, Parliament ordered it to be "slighted" and today only its impressive ruins remain. At *Kirby Muxloe* Lord Hastings began building his palatial fortified house, in dark red and blue brick, on the site of an earlier fourteenth century manor house of which very few traces remain. Work began in October 1480 and was brought to a premature close at the end of 1484,

Edward IV. In 1474, he received a royal licence to fortify three great houses in Leicestershire, at Ashby, Kirby, and Bagworth. However, little work was undertaken at Bagworth and building on a large scale was concentrated on the other two. In both cases, the buildings were designed as a combination of house and fortress, made necessary for rich and powerful men to protect themselves against the anarchy of the Wars of the Roses. At *Ashby* work began in 1474 on the site of a small fourteenth-century manor house, of which part still remains. The new work included a magnificent tower-house, originally 90 feet high with walls 9 feet thick. The house was contained within a garden whose walls and towers were of brick, the rest of the buildings being of stone quarried nearby. Thus Ashby is significant in being the earliest example of the use of bricks for building in Leicestershire since the departure of the Romans more than a thousand years before. The castle was altered in the late sixteenth or early seventeenth century and during

1. *(above) The ruins of Ashby Castle, dating mostly from the late fifteenth century.*

2. *(right) Ashby Castle, the impressive ruins of the Hastings Tower, originally 90 feet high.*

3. *The building of Kirby Muxloe Castle began in 1480 but was never completed. What remains today of the moated site are the gatehouse and the west tower. Gun-ports, among the earliest in the country, though probably only decorative, can also be seen.*

following the beheading of Lord Hastings in London the previous June. When Richard III succeeded to the throne in 1483, Hastings found himself on the wrong side and, having been denounced by the Duke of Gloucester as a traitor, was executed. Although the building was never completed, it remains one of the finest examples of late medieval brickwork in England. It is of considerable interest for another reason: its gun-ports are among the earliest in the country, though they may only have been decorative features as there is no record of guns having been ordered. Today, only the gatehouse and west tower stand.

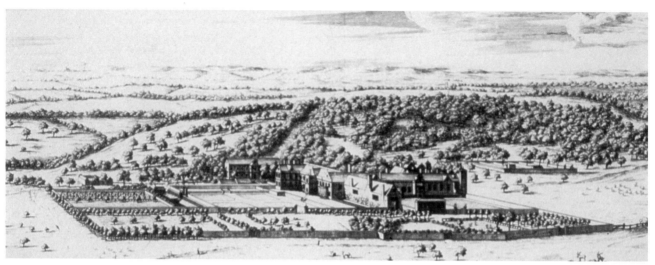

4. *(Above) This engraving of Bradgate House by Leonard Knyff dates from about 1700 and shows it while it was still occupied. Deserted in 1720, it gradually fell into ruin.*

Tudor Country Houses

The first true country house to be built in the two counties and, indeed, one of the earliest in the country, was at *Bradgate*. Bradgate Park began life as a typical medieval hunting park and, indeed the park today, though much enlarged, probably looks little different from its predecessor which was first recorded in 1241.[4] The park and the surrounding land came into the possession of Thomas Grey, first Marquis of Dorset, in 1475, who unlike his rival, Lord Hastings, found himself on the winning side once Henry VII came to the throne. Recent research suggests that he began building here about 1500 when he set a precedent followed by later landowners by depopulating the village of Bradgate and enclosing the land in his park. The house, constructed in brick, was only partially erected when the Marquis died in 1501 and the work was probably completed by his son, Thomas, the second Marquis, by the time of his death in 1530. The building was

5. *The ruins of Bradgate House today are set in a park which has changed little over the centuries.*

distinctive in being a non-fortified country house, reflecting the more stable society of the Tudor period. Over the centuries, the house was altered and added to and was occupied until about 1720 when Henry Grey, who by this time had become the third Earl of Stamford, had newly inherited the title. Bradgate by now was old-fashioned and in need of expensive restoration. Consequently, being resident in Enville Hall in Staffordshire, he decided to stay where he was and left the house unoccupied. As a result, it fell into disrepair and by the end of the eighteenth century had become a ruin.[5] So it remains today, redolent of past glories.

Another Leicestershire country house containing late fifteenth century work is *Nevill Holt,* in the south-eastern corner of the county. Not a completely new house like Bradgate, it evolved gradually over the centuries, so that at its core is a fourteenth century hall, with some fine late fifteenth century work attributed to Thomas Palmer, who died in 1474, and his Nevill son-in-law. The same is true of *Stapleford Park,* on the eastern edge of Leicestershire, where the earliest part of the present house was built in 1500 by Thomas Sherard, a wealthy squire. Subsequently, additions were made to the house in a variety of architectural styles, right up to the eighteenth century.

6. *The east wing of Stapleford Park, known as Lady Abigail's Wing, dates originally from 1500 and was reconstructed in 1633. Between the windows on the first floor are twelve niches containing statues, the six to the right dating from about 1500 and the six to the left from 1633.*

As Tudor England prospered economically through the sixteenth century, particularly from the conversion of peasant farming into sheep pastures involving the depopulation of villages and hamlets, so the nobility, gentry and wealthy merchants acquired land and built themselves houses. Some, particularly those close to Henry VIII, benefitted greatly from his dissolution of the monasteries between 1536 and 1539 which resulted in the lands and buildings of between 800 and 1,000 monasteries throughout the country being sold into their hands. Examples in Leicestershire include estates such as Stanford, acquired by the Caves, Rothley Temple by the Babingtons, and extensive lands by the Manners, Earls, later Dukes, of Rutland. Thomas Manners, the first Earl of Rutland, inherited Belvoir in 1525 and, being a personal friend of Henry VIII, in 1543 acquired monastic properties on a grand scale including, in Leicestershire, all the lands of the abbeys of Croxton, Owston and Garendon and the neighbouring Priory of Belvoir. He and his son largely rebuilt *Belvoir Castle* and turned it into one of the most splendid houses in Elizabethan England.[6] It was rebuilt yet again in the latter part of the seventeenth century and for the last time, in its present form, in the early nineteenth century. In Rutland, the equivalents of the Earls of Rutland were the Noels who purchased extensive ecclesiastical property in the county, including that at Brooke.[7] Many of the new owners of these lands erected houses which sometimes incorporated parts of

the monastery and to their new houses they often appended the term "abbey" or "priory". Two Leicestershire examples are Launde Abbey and Grace Dieu Priory. At *Grace Dieu,* John Beaumont of nearby Coleorton acquired the site of the priory and built himself a large house, probably between 1539 and 1552, incorporating much of the priory behind his Tudor brickwork. Very little of this house remains and 300 years later another house, *Grace Dieu Manor,* was built here, some distance away from its predecessor. At *Launde Abbey,* where there was not an abbey but a priory, the land was acquired by Thomas Cromwell who built a mansion in the ruins. The present house has been so much altered that it is not clear how much of the sixteenth-century building still stands. Another monastic site which came into private hands after the Dissolution was *Leicester Abbey,* then on the edge of the town and now the site of Abbey Park. A Tudor house was built here, though there is no unanimity as to its date of erection. Hoskins[8] says it was built in about 1562 by Henry, Earl of Huntingdon, out of old material on the site, while Pevsner[9] states that it dates from

7. *One of the few Tudor houses in Leicestershire was Cavendish House, now in the north-west corner of Abbey Park, Leicester. Built about 1600 from the remains of Leicester Abbey, it was burnt out in 1645 during the Civil War.*

about 1600. In any case, the house, known as *Cavendish House*, after William Cavendish, first Earl of Devonshire, who acquired it in 1613, was burnt and plundered by Royalist troops in 1645 and today only some of the ruins remain, on the western edge of Abbey Park. In Rutland, the Priory at *Brooke* was acquired by the Noels, a family with many branches. Here, Andrew Noel built a house adjacent to the Priory which soon became ruinous. In 1642, the house ceased to be the principal residence of the family, fell into disuse and was demolished by the end of the century. All that remains today are an octagonal stone gate lodge and an arched gateway.

Among houses built or rebuilt in the late sixteenth century are, or were, *Husbands Bosworth Hall*, in the extreme south of Leicestershire, *Kirby Bellars Hall*, near Melton Mowbray, and *Clipsham Hall* in Rutland. Husbands Bosworth Hall dates

from the late Middle Ages, to which a timber-framed addition was made in the late sixteenth century. Subsequently it was much altered in the late seventeenth century and again in the nineteenth century. Kirby Bellars Hall was in existence in the early seventeenth century, but was burnt down in the Civil War. Its owner, Sir Erasmus Fontaine, had it rebuilt at some time before his death in 1672, but it was later demolished. Clipsham Hall dates from 1582 when it was built in local stone. It was added to and much altered in the late nineteenth century.

Country Houses in the Seventeenth Century

The first half of the seventeenth century was a period of growing prosperity for landowners, as a result of considerable progress both in agricultural productivity and also in the extension of the cultivated area. This enabled the nobility and gentry of rural England at this time to build a number of fine country houses. In Leicestershire, they included Cotes, Elmesthorpe, Wistow, Edmondthorpe, Rothley, Ragdale, Quenby, Shenton and Carlton Curlieu; and in Rutland Exton Old Hall and Martinsthorpe. Elmesthorpe Hall, northeast of Hinckley, is another country house which has left little trace behind. It was probably built about 1610 by the Harringtons who owned the estate. It was then purchased in 1619 by Sir William Cockaigne, Lord Mayor of London. After his death, his son, Charles Cockaine, later Viscount Cullen, made Elmesthorpe his principal residence. According to Nichols, the hall was a very large and extensive

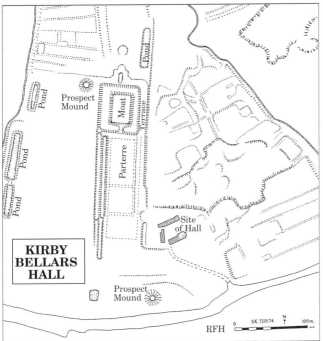

8. *The site of Kirby Bellars Hall, near Melton Mowbray. One of the grandest houses in Leicestershire, it was built in the early part of the seventeenth century, burnt down in the Civil War, rebuilt shortly after and subsequently demolished.*

Building Materials

Until the coming of the railways in the nineteenth century which made the transportation of building materials relatively easy, all but the grandest houses had to rely on what was locally available. Hence, country houses in the two counties were dependent on local geology for their building materials, which makes them fit so well into their surroundings.

Leicestershire, except for the eastern part of the county, is covered by Boulder Clay brought down by the ice sheets and underlain by heavy Lower Lias clays or deep red Triassic marls and what stone there is was either too deep to be accessible or in the case of Charnwood stone too hard to make for practicable working. Hence, inevitably, the principal building material for large houses – small ones relied on mud and timber – was brick, made from local clays. Although the Romans made brick in Leicester, as is illustrated by the second century Jewry Wall, once they departed the art of brick-making was lost and did not reappear until the 1470s and 1480s when bricks were made on site for the construction of *Ashby* and *Kirby Muxloe Castles*. These buildings embodied the typical *diapers* of the period, that is diamond-shaped panels of dark blue vitrified headers set against a red brick background. This style of brick building continued in Leicestershire into the early seventeenth century and is to be seen at *Quenby Hall*. Thereafter, the use of brick in western Leicestershire became widespread with the local clays and marls yielding bricks of a rich red colour. By the eighteenth century, most towns and villages in the county had their own brickyards supplying the basic building material for houses of various sizes. As a rule, the larger houses had stone dressings along the sides of the buildings and around the windows though, in practice, this stone weathered less well than the brick. Among the many fine brick mansions, with stone dressings, in western Leicestershire are *Market Bosworth Hall*, *Noseley Hall* and *Staunton Harold Hall*.

10. *and* 11. *Among the fine brick mansions in west Leicestershire are Market Bosworth Hall (above) and Staunton Harold Hall (below). The former, built at the end of the seventeenth century, has stone trimmings. The latter, an older house, was added to in the eighteenth century and this photograph show the south front of Lion Court, built in 1763, so-called because of the leaded lion perched above the parapet.*

9. *(left) Late fifteenth- and early sixteenth-century brick buildings were often decorated with diapers, diamond-shaped panels of dark-blue vitrified headers set against a red background, as here at Kirby Muxloe Castle.*

In eastern Leicestershire stone asserts itself, mainly in the form of the Middle Lias marlstone which because it contains iron oxide is commonly known as ironstone. It varies in colour from deep orange through rust-brown to a lighter golden brown. The characteristic building stone in this part of the country, it can be seen in village churches and in fine form in *Belvoir Castle* where, topped up with limestone dressings, it makes for an attractive combination of brilliant yellow and grey. Other east Leicestershire houses which have been built of marlstone, frequently like Belvoir with limestone dressings, include *Brooksby Hall, Cold Overton Hall, Langton Hall* and *Launde Abbey*. There is a small area of grey, oolitic limestone in the extreme north-eastern part of the county, but this beautiful stone is much more widely found in Rutland. The only other significant area of accessible stone in Leicestershire is in Charnwood Forest where some of the oldest rocks in the country rear up to nearly a thousand feet. However, these mainly volcanic rocks have been so hard to work until the nineteenth century that they have contributed hardly at all to the county's country houses. Throughout Leicestershire country houses were mainly roofed with Swithland slates, though more recently Welsh slates have been used.

13. *In Rutland, fine limestones are available for building. Here, at Burley-on-the-Hill, Ketton Stone was used, dug out from quarries in the village of that name not far away.*

12. *The eastern half of Leicestershire contains easily workable ironstone which is widely used in this part of the county for churches and country houses as here at Belvoir Castle, where it is topped up with limestone dressings.*

Rutland, by contrast, is particularly well endowed with stone for building materials, as virtually the whole county is underlain with Jurassic Limestone. In the western half this consists of a continuation of Leicestershire's golden brown ironstone, while the eastern half consists of Inferior Oolite, a grey limestone considered by many to be the most beautiful building stone in the country. Together, they make up part of the great Stone Belt which sweeps up from Dorset, through the Cotswolds, Northamptonshire, Rutland and Lincolnshire to Yorkshire. The oolite has always been more highly regarded than the marlstone because, beauty apart, it is more durable. Quarried at various places in the county, notably at Clipsham where it has a pale brown tinge and at Ketton where it is grey, it has been greatly in demand for centuries. Thus, Clipsham stone has been used extensively for Oxford colleges and Ketton stone at Cambridge. Both these fine limestones have been widely used in Rutland itself: for example *Burley-on-the-Hill* is built mainly of Clipsham stone with a colonnade of Ketton stone and *Clipsham Hall* is built of stone from its local quarry. Stone slates are plentifully available, mainly from Collyweston just across the border in Northamptonshire or from Swithland in Leicestershire.

Sources: This section has drawn largely on Alec Clifton-Taylor's sections on the Building Materials of Leicestershire and Rutland in Nikolaus Pevsner and Elizabeth Williamson, *The Buildings of England: Leicestershire and Rutland*, Penguin Books, Revised Edition, 1984.

building of which the remains of the porter's lodge were taken down in about 1750. *Cotes Hall*, to the east of Loughborough, was built by the Skipwith family about 1600 but was destroyed by fire in the eighteenth century. Today, all that remain are extensive earthworks which mark the remnants of the gardens which accompanied the Hall. *Wistow Hall* was probably built about 1603 for the Halford family on an H-plan typical of the period and was subsequently much altered in the late eighteenth and early nineteenth centuries. *Edmondthorpe Hall* was built in about 1621 by Roger Smith and also later much altered at a later date. The estate was purchased by the Pochins of Barkby Hall in 1762, who still own it, and the house was burnt down accidentally in 1942 when it was occupied by the Army. *Rothley Hall*, the home of the Babingtons for centuries, is now a hotel, Rothley Court. The house, of medieval origin, was largely remodelled in the early seventeenth century and altered in the eighteenth and nineteenth centuries. At *Ragdale*, the home of the Shirleys for four and a half centuries, a Tudor house was built about 1550, and then between 1629 and 1631 Sir Henry Shirley restored and greatly enlarged the house, still principally using brick. In due course it was turned into a farmhouse, abandoned in this century and demolished in 1958. According to Pevsner it was one of the finest sixteenth and seventeenth century houses in Leicestershire and should not have been allowed to

14. *Ragdale Old Hall, one of the finest fifteenth- and sixteenth-century houses in Leicestershire, was sadly demolished in 1958.*

16. *A drawing of Martinsthorpe House, near Manton, Rutland. Built in about 1622, it was demolished in 1755. The stables were converted into a house, known today as Old Hall Farm.*
(Reproduced with permission from Bryan Waites, 'A Celebration of Rutland', Multum in Parvo Press, 1994)

disappear.[10] All that remains today is a fireplsce and panelling which are housed in the Newarke House Museum in Leicester. *Quenby Hall* is a splendid early seventeenth century brick mansion, probably the finest of its time in Leicestershire, being built between 1618 and 1630 for George Ashby. *Shenton Hall*, on the south-western edge of Leicestershire, was built in Gothic style for William Wollaston and was completed in 1629. However, it was considerably altered in the nineteenth century and of the original early seventeenth century house only the gatehouse and the northwest front remain. *Carlton Curlieu Hall* was built in about 1636 for Sir John Bale and substantially remodelled later in the same century and again in the early nineteenth century. In Rutland, *Exton Old Hall* was built for the Noels in the early seventeenth century and burnt down in 1810. The ruins now stand near the New Hall which

dates from two periods in the nineteenth century. *Martinsthorpe House,* near Manton, south of Oakham, was built about 1622 for William Fielding. A magnificent mansion set in a park, it passed into the hands of the Duke of Devonshire in the 1750s and he ordered its demolition in 1755. Today, only the stables remain, converted into Old Hall Farm.

The Civil War put a stop to most building for a decade at least and, indeed, for most of the rest of the seventeenth century few country houses were built in the two counties, perhaps because, as Hoskins suggests[11], it took the great landowners a long time to recover from the ravages of the Civil War. However, one house that was probably built in the 1650s, was *Cold Overton Hall*, on the eastern edge of Leicestershire. Built for John St John, it was added to in the early nineteenth century and partly demolished in the First World War.

Towards the end of the seventeenth century, the building and enlarging of country houses in the

15. *The ruins of Exton Old Hall, Rutland. The home of the Noels, it was burnt it was burned down in 1810. A new large house was built bnearby the following year.*

17. *Stanford Hall, a fine William and Mary mansion on the southern edge of Leicestershire.*

two counties gathered momentum: examples include Lockington Hall, Market Bosworth Hall, Quorn Hall, Stanford Hall, Stapleford Hall and Stretton Hall in Leicestershire; and Burley-on-the- Hill and Lyndon Hall in Rutland. These houses were typically built in what Littlejohn[12] calls a "compact, rigorously symmetrical" style, of brick blocks edged in stone and topped by a single hipped roof, underlined by a broad, crisp cornice. In these respects, they marked a transitional architectural style leading to the eighteenth century which saw most of the fine building in the two counties. In chronological order, *Lyndon Hall*, just south of Rutland Water, was the first to be built, between 1671 and 1677. Built for Sir Abel Barker, it is a compact, absolutely square house, with a hipped roof. At *Stapleford Park*, in the 1670s, Bennet Sherard added to the existing house another one quite typical of the period. *Stretton Hall*, near Great Glen, south-east of Leicester, was probably built by George Hewett between 1670 and 1690. *Quorn Hall*, on the east side of the village, dates from about 1680 but has been much added to and altered, at the end of the eighteenth century and again a century later. *Lockington Hall* was originally built of stone in about 1688 and remodelled at the end of the eighteenth century. *Market Bosworth Hall*, a grand Baroque West Leicestershire house, was probably built by Sir Beaumont Dixie who died in 1692. Though much altered in the nineteenth century, it is still typical of the earlier period with its characteristic red brick and white stone dressing, pediment and giant pilasters. Then right at the end of the century, between 1696 and 1700, Daniel Finch, second Earl of Nottingham, built his great house at *Burley-on-the-Hill*. At about the same time, between about 1697 and 1703, Sir Roger Cave had *Stanford Hall,* the finest William and Mary house in the two counties, built right at the southern edge of Leicestershire.

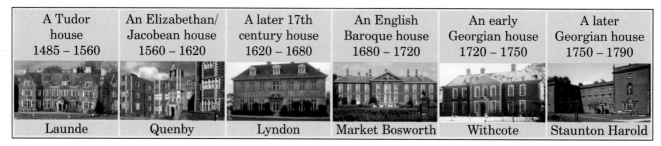

A Tudor house 1485 – 1560	An Elizabethan/ Jacobean house 1560 – 1620	A later 17th century house 1620 – 1680	An English Baroque house 1680 – 1720	An early Georgian house 1720 – 1750	A later Georgian house 1750 – 1790
Launde	Quenby	Lyndon	Market Bosworth	Withcote	Staunton Harold

Georgian Country Houses

The eighteenth century was the period par excellence for the building of country houses and Leicestershire and Rutland are fortunate in having a considerable legacy of fine Georgian buildings. In the early decades of the century, among the tasteful and dignified houses that went up are Lowesby Hall, Osbaston Hall, Withcote Hall, Belgrave Hall, Noseley Hall, Scraptoft Hall and Stretton Hall in Leicestershire, and Tickencote Hall in Rutland. *Lowesby Hall*, which like many other houses had an earlier core, was built of brick for Isaac Wollaston in 1707. The same is true of *Osbaston Hall* which although it incorporates an earlier house, to outward appearances dates from the early seventeenth century. *Withcote Hall,* was built of golden coloured stone for Matthew Johnson who died in 1723. *Belgrave Hall*, originally located in a country village to the north of Leicester but now firmly embedded in its suburbs, was built between 1709 and 1713 of red and dark blue brick for Edmund

Cradock. *Noseley Hall*, for centuries the home of the Hazlerigg family, was built for Sir Robert Hesilrige. Originally of brick, it was given a cement rendering in the late nineteenth century. *Scraptoft Hall,* now part of de Montfort University and like Belgrave Hall part of suburban Leicester, was an early seventeenth century manor house which was enlarged and completely remodelled for Lady Laetitia Wigley in

18. Withcote Hall, a delightful early Georgian Leicestershire house.

19. (opposite and below) Some examples of the major architectural styles

A Picturesque house 1790 – 1820	A Regency house about 1820	A neo-classical house about 1830	An early Victorian house 1840 – 1850	A later Victorian house 1850 – 1900	An Edwardian house 1902 – 1910
Donington	Quorn House	Ayston	Beaumanor	Ashby Folville	Papillon Hall

the 1720s. *Tickencote Hall*, in Rutland, was built in 1705 for the Wingfield family by the distinguished architect, Sir John Vanburgh. A fine typical Queen Anne two-storey stone house, with a pedimented centre and a steep hipped roof, it was sadly pulled down in about 1950.

Finally, mention must be made of two other fine Leicestershire houses built in the 1740s and both sadly lost: Garendon Hall and Gopsall Hall. *Garendon Hall* was built on the site of a twelfth century Cistercian monastery dissolved in 1536. Just to the west of Loughborough, it was a magnificent mansion erected for the Phillipps family in about the 1730s in a pure Palladian style, that is following the

20. *(above) Belgrave Hall, a red brick early eighteenth-century house. Originally in a village to the north of Leicester, it is now in its suburbs.*

21. *(right) Garendon Hall, near Loughborough, built in a Palladian style in about the 1730s and recast by the architect E. W. Pugin in the 1860s, it was demolished in 1964 and the rubble used in the construction of the nearby M1 motorway.*

22. *The Temple of Venus in Garendon Park, built between 1729 and 1739.*

examples and principles of Andrea Palladio, the sixteenth century Italian architect, and was recast by E.W. Pugin in the 1860s. In 1964, the house, empty and disused, was sold and demolished and the resulting rubble used as part of the M1 motorway, then under construction nearby. Although the house has gone, the parkland still contains probably the finest classical monuments in Leicestershire. Designed by Ambrose Phillipps, between 1729 and 1739, they include the Temple of Venus, the Triumphal Arch and the Obelisk.

Gopsall Hall, near Twycross, described by Pevsner as "the most expensive and lavishly decorated" eighteenth century house in Leicestershire[13], was built between 1747

23. *Gopsall Hall, near Twycross, one of the grandest houses in Leicestershire. Built between 1747 and 1749 and set in a large park, it was badly damaged by the Army in the Second World War and demolished in 1951.*

and 1749 and set in a large park. It was built for Charles Jennens who inherited a large fortune made by Birmingham ironmasters and who was reputed to have spent 100,000 pounds – an enormous sum by today's standards – on erecting the house. It was designed by a local architect, Alderman John Westley of Leicester. It came to Earl Howe in the early nineteenth century, in whose family's hands it remained until 1919 when it was purchased by Lord Waring. However, he never lived here and after his death the estate was sold, in 1927. The house was used by the Army during the Second World War and after the war was left to fall into ruin until, in 1951, what was left of its contents were sold off and the buildings were razed to the ground.[14] Today, scarcely a trace of this once grand house remains.

Another great house of the same period which has been pulled down was *Normanton Hall*, in Rutland. Situated on what is now the southern shore of Rutland Water, it was built for Sir Gilbert Heathcote between about 1735 and 1740, and altered and enlarged between 1763 and 1767. At the same time, Heathcote depopulated the village of Normanton in order to create a park round his hall. The house was demolished in 1925 but the stables and some farm buildings survive in what Pevsner calls "a sound and pleasant neo-classical style".[15]

24. *Gumley Hall, south of Leicester, lasted for exactly 200 years. Begun in 1764, it was demolished in 1964.*

During the latter part of the eighteenth century, country houses were, if anything, built or rebuilt on straighter and plainer lines than earlier in the century, constituting what their owners called "neat residences".[16] Among them, in Leicestershire, are, or were, Gumley, Baggrave, Braunstone and Staunton Harold and Wistow Halls. *Gumley Hall*, on the southern edge of Leicester, is yet another country house we have lost. It was begun on a new site in 1764 for Joseph Cradock, a friend of Dr Johnson and Garrick, whose family had accumulated considerable wealth in trade in Leicester. It was of brick and consisted of seven bays with a three-bay pediment and a Tuscan colonnade which was added in 1869-70, and set in fashionable pleasure grounds. Requisitioned by the Army during the War, for some time afterwards it was used partly as flats for ex-servicemen and partly as a warehouse.[17] Although, sadly, it was demolished in 1964, much of the park remains with woods and lakes and earthworks of the formal gardens.

Baggrave Hall dates originally from the sixteenth century but was rebuilt in the 1750s along plain Georgian lines for John Edwyn. *Braunstone Hall*, once in the country but now in the south-western suburbs of Leicester, was built in brick in 1776 for Clement Winstanley and set in parkland. The Winstanley estate was purchased by the Borough of Leicester in 1925 mainly for housing and some of the parkland, containing the house, was set aside as a public park. *Staunton Harold Hall*, the home of the Shirley family for centuries, dates back to the fifteenth century and parts of the original house are embedded in the present building which was mainly erected in the 1760s. *Wistow Hall* probably dates from the beginning of the seventeenth century. However, it was modernised in the late eighteenth century by Sir William Halford and given a Gothic facade in the early nineteenth century.[18]

At the end of the eighteenth century, architectural styles changed yet again and "picturesque" buildings came into vogue. The "Picturesque" style adopted by architects like John Nash and landscape designers like Humphry Repton

25. *The porch on the main front of Donington Hall, Leicestershire. The house was built at the end of the eighteenth century in a romantic 'Gothic' style.*

Donington Hall in north-west Leicestershire built between 1790 and 1793 in the style known as Strawberry Hill Gothic, after Horace Walpole's eccentric house at Strawberry Hill, near Twickenham. It was built for Francis Rawdon Hastings to the design of William Wilkins and at the same time the park was landscaped by the celebrated landscape designer, Humphry Repton.

Country Houses in the Nineteenth Century

Another Picturesque building of the beginning of the nineteenth century is the Duke of Rutland's *Belvoir Castle*, romantically perched on its hilltop and evoking the Middle Ages. Begun in 1801, it was not until 1830 that the building was completed. A more widely popular architectural style of this period is Neo-Classical and several Leicestershire houses were constructed in this fashion. The grandest of them was *Buckminster Park* on the north-eastern edge of the county. Designed by Samuel Saxon for Sir

26. *Buckminster Park, Leicestershire, near the Lincoln-shire border, was a grand late eighteenth century house built in a Neo-Classical style. It was demolished in 1952.*

applied to the total appearance of a building in its setting. As far as buildings were concerned, its major features were a liking for castellations, Gothic and Italian or "Old English" styles.[19] A typical example is

William Manners, it was erected between 1793 and 1798, and demolished in 1952. The park was landscaped by Humphry Repton and some of his landscaping remains as do the large stables. Two houses built in a similar style at the turn of the nineteenth century are Whatton House and Coleorton Hall. *Whatton House*, near Long Whatton in the north of Leicestershire, was designed for Edward Dawson and dates from about 1802, though the present house acquired its appearance from an extensive remodelling which took place after a fire in 1876. *Coleorton Hall* was built between 1804 and 1808 for Sir George Beaumont, in a classically severe style, and enlarged in 1862.

In the first half of the nineteenth century, landowners continued to build or rebuild their houses, among them Skeffington Hall, Barkby Hall, Burleigh Hall, Quorn House, Swithland Hall, Grace Dieu Manor, Prestwold Hall and Beaumanor Park. *Skeffington Hall*, dating from various periods from the late fifteenth century, was substantially altered about 1800 and again between 1843 and 1850 by the Skeffington family who had lived there throughout this long period. *Barkby Hall*, the home of the Pochins, dates from the first half of the sixteenth century; however, it was rebuilt about 1810 and altered later in the nineteenth century. *Burleigh Hall,* its estate now the campus of Loughborough University, dated from the second half of the seventeenth century. However, it was remodelled and given a new classical exterior early in the nineteenth century. It was purchased by Alderman Harold Coltman in 1919 and he lived here until his death shortly before 1959 when it was purchased by the Ministry of Education for what is now the University. It was demolished in 1961.

Quorn House, just to the west of the centre of the village, was built for the Farnham family in about 1820, in a plain style in its park, which centuries before had been a mediaeval hunting park. *Swithland Hall*, was built for the Earl of Lanesborough in a Greek Revival style between the 1830s and the 1850s. It replaced an older hall which burnt down in 1822, but on a new site.

27. *The south front of Quorn House, with its shallow brick bays, typical of the 1820s when it was built.*

Prestwold Hall, like many houses, was built and altered at different periods from the early seventeenth century onwards. However, it acquired its present appearance when it was made "fashionably Italianate"[20] in 1842. *Grace Dieu Manor*, designed by William Railton, was built in 1833-4, in a Tudor-Gothic style for Ambrose March Phillipps de Lisle, whose family seat at Garendon was occupied by his father. Railton also designed

Beaumanor Park for the very wealthy Robert Herrick. Built in a sumptuous Jacobean style between 1842 and 1845, it replaced an eighteenth century classical mansion, considered by Nichols in his History of Leicestershire to be "very dismal", demolished a few years earlier. *Ayston Hall* in Rutland, just north of Uppingham, is an older house which was given a new plain front in 1807

Historic Houses on the Same Site

A number of country houses in Leicestershire have been built and rebuilt a number of times on the same site. Good examples include Beaumanor Park, Belvoir Castle and Donington Hall. The first house at *Beaumanor Park*, near Loughborough, was certainly in existence in the early fourteenth century, being rebuilt by Henry Beaumont in 1327. It subsequently passed through several hands, including the Greys of Bradgate, until it was purchased by Sir William Herrick in 1595. By now, it was probably in a dilapidated state and Herrick immediately set about altering it. However, it is not known whether any parts of the medieval house survived or, indeed, if the newer house was on the same site as its predecessor. A Jacobean mansion in appearance, the new house is shown in a print in Nichols' *History and Antiquities of the County of Leicester*, III, 1800, p.147

and a survey of the Manor of Beaumanor dated 1656 describes it as having "a very fair and clear moat" around it. Inside, the house was arranged around a courtyard. By the beginning of the eighteenth century, it was considered old-fashioned and was almost certainly in need of repair. A new house was built on the site, between 1726 and 1735, on pure classical lines. Finally, in 1842, William Perry Herrick demolished the Georgian house and began building the present one.

The present *Belvoir Castle* is the fourth one on the same site. The first, a Norman castle, was built at the end of the eleventh century, to be replaced by a grand Tudor mansion in the sixteenth century. Following the latter's

demolition in the Civil War, a new house was built in a classical style between 1655 and 1668. This was replaced by the present house at the beginning of the nineteenth century. *Donington Hall* has been built and rebuilt at least three times. The first building was a manor house, possibly medieval in origin, replaced by a rambling hall to which an extension was added in the eighteenth century. The present Hall was built between 1790 and 1793.

28. *(above) The early seventeenth-century Beaumanor Hall, as shown in Nichols' 'History of Leicestershire', 1800.*
29. *(top right) This print of Belvoir Castle from J. Throsby's 'Select Views of Leicestershire' (1790) shows the classical house completed in the 1660s.*
30. *(right) This view of Donington Hall taken from Nichols shows it as it was in the late eighteenth century shortly before its rebuilding, a rambling building of various ages.*

For much of the nineteenth century, as the British Empire grew and flourished, so for the most part landowners became more wealthy and the traditional holders of estates, the nobility and gentry, were increasingly joined by manufacturers and merchants who having found wealth in the cities purchased estates and built themselves houses in the country. This process had, of course, been going on for centuries as is exemplified by Charles Jennens who, as we have seen, built Gopsall Hall in the 1750s from his inheritance of the fortune made by Birmingham ironmasters. Similarly, in 1872 James Alexander Jackson, a Liverpool cotton broker had the lavish *Thurnby Court* built. With rooms with painted ceilings and murals by Italian artists, it cost 250,000 pounds to build and equip. The Jacksons lived here for little more than 20 years after which it stood empty until it was bought for 6,000 pounds by a Mr Heath who demolished it in 1916. A long-established landowner, the Earl of Stamford, built himself an extensive mansion in the shape of *Bradgate House*, the second one to carry the name but located some distance away from the original in Bradgate Park being situated at Stewards Hay, near Groby. Built in 1856, it became too expensive to maintain and was demolished in 1925. Another vast, largely Victorian, house was *Stoughton Grange*. To a much older house, the Powys-Keck family who inherited the estate in 1860 added an Elizabethan Gothic northwest front of stone and on the southeast side an Italianate red brick range with spired towers at each end. In 1913, the estate was sold by auction but there were no takers for the house which stood empty until 1926 when in Pevsner's words "this monster" was demolished.[21] Part of the estate was purchased by the Wholesale Cooperative Society in 1919 on which the present Stoughton Park Farm stands. One late Victorian house in Leicestershire that has survived is *Ashby Folville Manor*, rebuilt in 1893.

The Decline of the Country House in the Twentieth Century

As is only too evident, the twentieth century has witnessed enormous changes in the ownership and, indeed, in the very existence of the nation's country houses. These changes can be said to date mainly from about 1879 when the great Agricultural Depression began , with the importation of vast quantities of cheap grain from the United States and Russia. As a consequence, the value of agricultural land in England dropped by a third by the end of the century and the economic base upon which the great estates depended was undermined. The country house was the centre of a prosperous agricultural estate and once revenues began to decline it became increasingly difficult to staff and maintain it. The situation was made worse by the fearful loss of young males of the landed classes in the First World War and the toll of death duties which rose from 8 per cent in 1904 to 50 per cent in the 1930s. As a result, scarcely a new country house has been built in the two counties in the present century, one of the few exceptions being *Papillon Hall* , at Lubenham near, Market Harborough. Built between 1902 and 1904 by the distinguished architect Sir Edwin Lutyens for Frank Belville, manufacturer of Robinson's Barley Water, it replaced a seventeenth century house built for a Huguenot engineer named David Papillon. Lutyens designed it on a butterfly plan so that its name is a pun, as 'papillon' means butterfly in French. It was also distinguished by having a garden designed by Gertrude Jekyll. Occupied by the military during the Second World War, it was demolished in 1950.

Long before that, indeed from the later nineteenth century onwards, the major demolition of country houses began. One reason was the relentless spread of the city of Leicester which led to the destruction of Danets Hall and Westcotes Hall in the latter part of the nineteenth century and Birstall Hall and Humberstone Hall in the early twentieth century. *Danets Hall* was an old house rebuilt in about 1700. It passed through a variety of hands until its last owner died of cholera in 1861. The estate was then sold for building purposes and the house demolished; today, Dannett Street near Black Friars marks its approximate site. *Westcotes Hall*, an older house, refronted about 1730, was the home of the Ruding family from the mid-sixteenth century until 1821 when it passed into other hands. The estate was sold for building purposes in 1886 and the house pulled down. Cranmer Street, just off the Narborough Road, marks the approximate site of the house. *Birstall Hall* dated from about 1764 and was enlarged in the early nineteenth century. It passed through various hands until about 1914 after which it stood empty. It was demolished in 1923 and the estate was built over.[22] *Humberstone Hall*, was an older house much developed by the Paget banking family in the late nineteenth century. The house and estate were sold for building purposes in 1919 and although the house was divided into flats at that time it was demolished four years later.[23]

The rate of loss of country houses greatly accelerated in the inter-war years for the reasons already described: the continued depression in land values, the loss of heirs in the Great War coupled with the growth to record levels of income and inheritance tax, the difficulty in finding enough servants to run the houses, and the problem of finding new owners or new uses. Consequently, over 450 substantial British country houses were lost between the wars[24], among them *Stoughton Grange* and *Bradgate House* in Leicestershire and *Normanton Hall* in Rutland. The situation was made much worse when, during the Second World War, the government requisitioned almost all our country houses for use as hospitals, boarding schools, and occupation by the services. In the process many country houses were very badly treated by their occupants: in Leicestershire, for example, *Edmondthorpe Hall* was burned down by accident in 1942, when occupied by the Army; *Garendon Hall*, also occupied by the Army, was so badly treated that afterwards it was virtually uninhabitable; and *Beaumanor Park* and *Donington Hall* were, at the very least, neglected, if not seriously damaged. As a result of their treatment during the war, many country houses proved incapable of restoration once it was over. Thus, of the thousand or so country houses demolished throughout the country in the decade after the ending of the Second World War, nearly all can be described as "delayed war losses".[25] In some ways Leicestershire and Rutland got off relatively lightly; however, among those lost in the 20 years after the war were *Papillon* in 1950, *Tickencote* in about 1950, *Gopsall* in 1951, *Buckminster* in 1952, *Ragdale* in 1958, *Burleigh* in 1961 and *Garendon* and *Gumley* in 1964.

During the 1960s country houses throughout the country were overlooked or neglected by successive governments and their upkeep was becoming increasingly expensive and difficult, so that by the 1970s their future looked grim. Indeed, at that time the idea of a wealth tax was being strongly mooted and its introduction would have had a very harmful effect on our country houses and their owners. It was to counteract this threat that the Historic Houses Association (HHA) was formed in 1973. Since then, it has been very successful in campaigning on behalf of country house owners to whom it offers guidance and help on matters like tourism and marketing, security, insurance and taxation, and technical matters such as planning and grants. It currently has about 1,400 members throughout the United Kingdom, including a

Country Houses We Have Lost

Over the centuries, many country houses have disappeared, for many reasons. From time to time, their owners found them too difficult, too expensive, or simply inconvenient to maintain and had them pulled down or allowed them to fall into ruin. Two examples are *Bradgate Park*, abandoned by the Earl of Stamford in 1720 and *Martinsthorpe*, near Manton in Rutland, which was demolished in 1755 by order of the

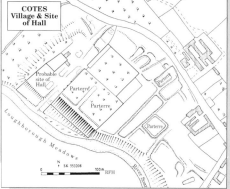

Duke of Devonshire. Fire has always been a hazard, sometimes disastrously so, and houses that have been burnt down include *Cotes Hall*, near Loughborough, in the eighteenth century, *Exton Old Hall*, in 1810, and *Edmonthorpe Hall*, as a consequence of military occupation, in 1942.

The loss of country houses greatly accelerated after the middle of the nineteenth century. One of the main reasons for this, in Leicestershire, was the relentless spread of the city of Leicester. This led to the destruction of *Danets Hall*, and *Westcotes Hall* in the city, in 1861 and about 1886 respectively, and *Birstall Hall*, on its northern edge, demolished in 1923, and *Humberstone Hall*, on its eastern

31. *(top) Cotes Hall, near Loughborough, was built by the Skipwiths about 1600 and destroyed by fire in the eighteenth century. This drawing shows the site of the Hall and the extensive gardens which accompanied it.*
32. *(far left) Edmondthorpe Hall in east Leicestershire was burned down by accident in 1942 when occupied by the Army.*
33. *(below right) Tickencote Hall, Rutland. This fine house, built by Sir John Vanburgh in 1705 for the Wingfield family, was pulled down in the 1950s.*
34. *(below) Danets Hall as shown by Nichols at the end of the 18th century. Then in the countryside, it was overtaken by the spread of the City of Leicester and demolished in the second half of the last century.*

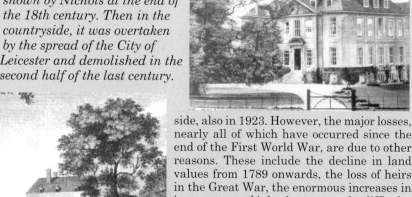

side, also in 1923. However, the major losses, nearly all of which have occurred since the end of the First World War, are due to other reasons. These include the decline in land values from 1789 onwards, the loss of heirs in the Great War, the enormous increases in income tax and inheritance tax, the difficulty in finding servants to run the houses, and the problems of finding new owners or uses. For all these reasons, Leicestershire and Rutland, like every other county in England, have lost many houses, some of them of considerable architectural and historical distinction. Two fine architects whose houses have disappeared are Sir John Vanburgh, whose *Tickencote Hall* in Rutland, built in 1765, was pulled down in the 1950s and

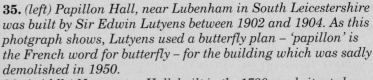

35. *(left) Papillon Hall, near Lubenham in South Leicestershire was built by Sir Edwin Lutyens between 1902 and 1904. As this photgraph shows, Lutyens used a butterfly plan – 'papillon' is the French word for butterfly – for the building which was sadly demolished in 1950.*
36. *(middle) Normanton Hall, built in the 1730s and situated on what is now the southern shore of Rutland Water, was demolished in 1926.*
37. *(bottom) Burleigh Hall, situated on what is now the campus of Loughborough University,was built in the second half of the seventeenth century, remodelled at the beginningof the nineteenth century, and pulled down in 1961.*

Sir Edwin Lutyens, whose Papillon Hall, near Lubenham, in Leicestershire, built between 1902 and 1904, and with a garden planted by Gertrude Jekyll in 1903, was demolished in 1950. Two huge, largely Victorian houses, of no great architectural merit perhaps but interesting nevertheless, and hugely inconvenient by more recent standards, were Thurnby Court, to the east of 1872 and demolished in 1916, and Stoughton Grange, to the south-east of Leicester, mainly of 1882-3 and demolished in 1926. Another lost, large house, of considerably greater historical and architectural merit was *Normanton Hall* in Rutland. Standing on what is now the southern shore of Rutland Water, it was built between 1733 and 1740 and pulled down in 1926.

During the Second World War, many country houses were requisitioned by the Services and some of them were so badly treated that they were demolished in the post-war period. They include the great house at *Gopsall*, demolished in 1951, and *Garendon Park*, pulled down in 1964 and the rubble used as foundation during the building of the nearby M1 motorway. Other fine houses which have gone since the end of the war include *Ragdale Old Hall*, one of the finest sixteenth to seventeenth century houses in Leicestershire, demolished in 1958, *Burleigh Hall* on what is now the campus of Loughborough University, built in the second half of the seventeenth century

and demolished in 1961, *Gumley Hall* begun in 1764 and demolished in 1964, and *Cottesmore Hall*, in Rutland, Tudor in origin and the last major country house to be pulled down in the two counties, in 1974.

The lost houses listed here are but a proportion of those that have gone over the centuries; thus, J. D. Bennett in his book "Vanished Houses of Leicestershire" lists no fewer than 31 in that county alone. Fortunately, in 1975, the government of the day introduced legislation aimed at helping to preserve the remaining country houses and, since then, planning regulations have arrested their disappearance. Nevertheless, given the high cost of maintaining the buildings and other problems which they face, the future of our country houses is by no means secure and other losses may occur.

number in the two counties. Happily, the doom-laden forecasts made in the early 1970s were not been borne out by events. The tide was turned when, at this time, planning regulations were introduced which made it virtually impossible to tear town a country house of any substantial architectural or artistic merit. Unfortunately, these regulations were not in time to save *Cottesmore Hall*, in Rutland, which dated back to Tudor times. Seriously damaged by fire in 1926, it was reconstructed and after years of standing empty was pulled down in 1974. Then, in 1975, the Labour government introduced a system known as 'Conditional Exemption' by which historic country houses could be exempted from death duties subject to reasonable public access. Finally, what has been dubbed "the Stately Home Industry" got under way and increasing numbers of owners resorted to opening their houses to the public as a means of raising money to preserve them. Two obvious examples in Leicestershire are *Belvoir Castle* and *Stanford Hall*.

Nevertheless, the cost of maintaining and repairing large country houses is very considerable and for this and other reasons many houses in the two counties have passed out of their owners' hands and have been put to other uses. Thus, *Donington Hall* is now the headquarters of British Midland Airways, *Bosworth Hall* and *Stapleford Hall* are hotels, *Launde Abbey* is a retreat and study centre for the Anglican diocese of Leicester, *Scraptoft Hall* is a campus of de Montfort University, *Staunton Harold Hall* a home run by the Sue Ryder

Foundation and *Burley-on-the-Hill* has been converted into private apartments. However, a majority of the country houses in the two counties remain in private hands, some still in the ownership of families who have lived there for centuries, including the Pochins at *Barkby Hall*, the Manners at *Belvoir Castle*, the Hazleriggs at *Noseley Hall*, the Packe-Drury-Lowes at *Prestwold Hall, the* Caves at *Stanford Hall*, and the Noels at *Exton Hall*.

What of the future for our country houses? Given the high costs of maintenance and repair, for many it must remain precarious, especially for those in private hands. Indeed, as the Director-General of the Historic Association has recently put it, "The major problem facing every owner is keeping the roof on"[25]. In order to do so many owners have been forced to sell works of art to raise the money to preserve the fabric of their houses. It is also likely, therefore, that an increasing number will be put to other uses such as those listed above. Littlejohn[26] considers that the most likely uses will be as retirement and nursing homes and what he calls "multiple residences", as in the case of *Burley-on-the-Hill*. Others will become hotels, hospitals and educational establishments. However, to whatever uses they may be put in the future, our country houses are an abiding source of interest to the public and in terms of their contribution to our architectural and artistic heritage, the splendid park landscapes which often surround them and their historical associations, we must surely ensure that the best of them are preserved for posterity?

PART TWO
The Historic Country Houses of
Leicestershire And Rutland:
A Gazetteer

Belvoir Castle

Melton

Goadby Marwood Hall

Lockington Hall

Donington Park

Whatton House

Buckminster Park

Staunton Harold Hall

Garendon Hall

Prestwold Hall

Ragdale Old Hall

MELTON MOWBRAY

Edmondthorpe Hall

Coleorton Hall

LOUGHBOROUGH

Cotes Hall

Kirby Bellars Hall

Stapleford Park

Clipsham Hall

Grace Dieu Manor

Burleigh Hall

Ashby Castle

ASHBY -DE-LA-ZOUCH

Beaumanor Park

Quorn Hall

Quorn House

Brooksby Hall

Rutland

N. W. Leics.

Swithland Hall

Charnwood

Gaddesby Hall

Cottesmore Hall

Exton Hall

Rothley Court

Ashby Folville Manor

Cold Overton Old Hall

Langham Old Hall

Exton Old Hall

Tolethorpe Hall

Bradgate Park

Birstall

Barkby

Baggrave Hall

Lowesby Hall

Burley-on- the Hill

Tickencote Hall

Belgrave Hall

Humberstone Hall

Withcote

OAKHAM

Hambleton Old Hall

Gopsall Park

Kirby Muxloe Castle

Danets Hall

Scraptoft Hall

Quenby Hall

Brooke Priory

Hambleton Hall

Osbaston Hall

Cavendish House

Westcotes

Thurnby Court

Ingarsby Old Hall

Launde Abbey

Normanton

Lyndon Hall

Market Bosworth Hall

Braunstone Hall

Leicester

Stoughton Grange

Skeffington Hall

Keythorpe Hall

Martinsthorpe Hall

North Luffenham Hall

Shenton Hall

Oadby & Wigston

Stretton Hall

Noseley Hall

Ayston Hall

South Luffenham Hall

Hinckley & Bosworth

Elmesthorpe Hall

Blaby

Wistow Hall

Carlton Curlieu Hall

Nevill Holt Hall

HINCKLEY

Langton Hall

Harborough

Gumley Hall

Peatling Parva Hall

Papillon Hall

MARKET HARBOROUGH

Country Houses Mentioned in this Book
● *Existing Country Houses*
○ *Country Houses we have lost*

Husbands Bosworth Hall

N

KILOMETRES
0 2 4 6 8 10

0 2 4 6
MILES

Stanford Hall

Leicestershire

ASHBY FOLVILLE MANOR

Situated eight miles north-east of Leicester, the original manor house was built in the mid-seventeenth century on an H-plan. Having burnt down, it was rebuilt in 1893 in a similar style, to the designs of J. Eley. Built of coursed and squared ironstone with limestone ashlar dressings, it is of three storeys and attics, and consists of five bays. The west front has a three-bay recessed centre with a two-storey tower porch flanked by taller gabled wings. The central arched doorway has a shield panel above it dated 1893. According to Pevsner, the north side is essentially part of the original house, though much altered. The house is owned by Mr and Mrs Rimmington, Mrs Rimmington's professional name being Rosemary Conley.

38. Ashby Folville Manor. The original manor house having been burnt down, this one was rebuilt in 1893 in a mid-seventeenth-century style. This photograph shows the west front.

BAGGRAVE HALL

What one sees today is a plain mid-Georgian country house set in a small park in a green valley, south of South Croxton. The valley once contained a village which lay to the south of the house and which was deserted in about 1500. In the earlier part of sixteenth century, there was a house on this site, the property of Leicester Abbey, which as at nearby Ingarsby presumably dispossessed the villagers in order to lay down the land to sheep farming. After the Dissolution, in 1543, the manor of Baggrave came to Francis Cave, a relation of the Caves of Stanford Hall and at some time in the seventeenth century a wing was added. The house came to John Edwyn in 1680 and it was his ancestor, another John Edwyn, who largely rebuilt the house in the 1750s. Finally, a second wing was added, dated 1776. John Edwyn's daughter carried the estate to the Burnaby family who held it until 1939 when it

39. *The mid-Georgian west front of Baggrave Hall with its central three-bay section topped by a pediment with an oval bull's eye window.*

was sold. Since then, it has passed through various hands including those of Asil Nadir, the Turkish Cypriot entrepreneur.

The west front of the house, which faces the road through the park, is characteristically mid-Georgian and consists of seven bays and two storeys with quoins and a central section of three bays carrying a pediment with an oval bull's eye window with a carved stone frame. To the left is a more recent brick range. The house has a Swithland slate hipped roof with brick ridge stacks which are also hipped. The south front of five bays is quite plain, while on the north side there is some evidence of the sixteenth century house. Inside, the best rooms are the oak room in the south-east part of the house with its pedimented doorcases, panelling and overmantel; and the drawing room in the south-west of the house with its painted panelling and richly carved fireplace and overmantel in a style described by Pevsner "as a very rare mid-eighteenth century essay in the Jacobean Revival". To the east of the house are mid-eighteenth century stables with a walled kitchen garden beyond.

BARKBY HALL

*T*he manor of Barkby, some five miles north-east of Leicester, has been associated with the Pochin family for centuries and, indeed, they are still here. They are first mentioned in connection with Barkby in the fifteenth century and at some later date built a house here. It was rebuilt about 1810, damaged by fire in 1847 and altered again and considerably reduced in size in 1870. Even so, it remains a substantial building, two-and-a-half storeys tall and with a balustraded porch over the central two bays. The interior dates from the Regency and, although plain, has a grand staircase.

40. *The entrance front of Barkby Hall, eight bays wide, and with a two-bay balustraded porch.*

BEAUMANOR PARK

*A*s we have seen, over a period of at least 500 years some four houses were built in succession at Beaumanor, south of Loughborough. The last and present one dates from 1842 when building began. By this time, the estate had come into the hands of William Perry Herrick, one of the wealthiest of Victorian landowners owning large areas of land. Having ordered the demolition of the Georgian house, he commissioned William Railton to design and build him a new one. Railton, a fashionable London architect of the time had designed Nelson's column and also had local connections having, some ten years earlier, built Grace Dieu Manor for Ambrose Phillips de Lisle, Possibly influenced by having seen a drawing of the earlier Jacobean mansion at Beaumanor, he built the new house, which took until 1853 to complete, in a Victorian-Jacobean

41. *The entrance front of Beaumanor Park, a house built in the 1840s in a Victorian-Jacobean style.*

style in the form of a square of red brick with stone dressings. Of two storeys with shaped gables, three on each facade, it has a plain tile roof with tall brick stacks in clusters. The entrance front of three large gables has a slightly projecting central section with a round arched doorway with rusticated stone surrounds and a semi-circular oriel window above. Five stone steps lead up to a pair or richly carved oak doors.

Inside, the chief feature is the spacious central hall, with its intricately carved oak staircase and behind it a huge stained glass window of 21 armorial panels. In 1915 the last of the Perry Herrick family died and the estate passed out of their hands. The house was requisitioned for military purposes during the Second World War and was acquired by the Ministry of Defence in 1946. It was sold to Leicestershire County Council in 1974 who opened it three years later as a conference centre for teachers.

Sources: Pamela Drinkall, *A Brief History of Beaumanor Hall and Park*, Leicestershire Education Committee, 1978, and Caroline Wessell, *Portrait of Beaumanor*, Herricks and Beaumanor Society, 1988.

BELGRAVE HALL

*L*ying in a pleasant side street off the busy A6 on the northern edge of Leicester, Belgrave Hall when it was built by Edmund Cradock between 1709 and 1713 was located in a small village north of the city. In the almost three centuries of its existence it has passed through various hands, including the Vann family who lived there from 1767 to 1844 and ran a successful hosiery business from the Hall. It was then purchased by John Ellis MP and members of the Ellis family lived there until 1933 when it was acquired by Thomas Morley who sold it in 1936 to the Leicester City Council, since when it has been a museum. The house is of brick, with its west-facing front facade having a chequer pattern of red and dark blue. It consists of three storeys with a triple-pitched roof behind a plain facade and comprises three sections, each of two bays, with the narrower centre section recessed and with a doorway with a pediment. Behind the house is a formal garden with substantial parts of the original eighteenth-century garden remaining, divided into consecutive walled sections.

Source: *Belgrave Hall and Gardens*, Leicestershire Museums, Arts and Record Service, n.d.

42. *The garden front of Belgrave Hall, an early eighteenth-century house on the northern edge of Leicester.*

BELVOIR CASTLE

The present Belvoir Castle is the fourth house to be built on its commanding site on top of an escarpment overlooking the Vale of Belvoir, in the north-east corner of the county. It began life as a Norman castle erected by Robert de Todeni, William the Conqueror's standard bearer, at the end of the eleventh century. de Todeni's coffin lies in the chapel of the present building. The castle, which seems to have consisted of a rectangular keep surrounded by a massive wall, was damaged during the fighting in the Wars of the Roses in the 1470s and came into the hands of Lord Hastings who used some of the materials from the castle to build his own huge fortress-cum-house at Ashby. Inherited in a ruinous condition by Thomas Manners first Earl of Rutland in 1525, he and his son largely rebuilt the house so that by the time it was completed in 1555 it had become one of the most splendid houses in England.

Following its demolition at the end of the Civil War, work began on a new house in 1655 which was completed in 1668 in a classical style. Around it over the next thirty years or so were created terrace gardens, avenues and plantations. Nothing now remains of this house except a wooden model in the ballroom of the present house.

The fourth and final house, built of yellow ironstone with grey oolitic limestone dressings, is an early nineteenth century romantic vision of a medieval fortress. Designed by James Wyatt for John Henry Manners, fifth Duke of Rutland, work began in 1801, soon after the young Duke's twenty-first birthday. Wyatt worked on the house until his death in 1813, by which time two of the main fronts and many interiors had been completed. Three years later, a fire destroyed most of the interior work and the baton was picked up by the family chaplain, the Reverend Sir John Thoroton, who designed the reconstructed house, with the Duchess of Rutland, a keen amateur architect, being closely involved. The building was finally completed in 1830 in a style which Pevsner calls "Mixed Medieval" with its collection of towers, turrets, battlements and buttresses.

The interior rooms are

43. *Belvoir Castle, the early nineteenth-century conception of a medieval fortress, with its turrets and crenellations, built of orange-yellow ironstone with limestone dressings.*

spacious, not to say cavernous. Perhaps the most splendid is the 131-feet long Regent's Gallery, named in honour of a royal visit in 1814. Designed by Wyatt, it survived the fire of 1816 and is situated on the south-west front with a huge central bay occupying the Castle's round tower. Lined with marble busts on pedestals by Joseph Nollekens and hung with eighteenth century Gobelin tapestries and gilded mirrors, it is redolent of the early nineteenth century. Another striking room is the Elizabethan-style Salon designed by Matthew Cotes Wyatt, son of James Wyatt, at the behest of the Duchess of Rutland, and decorated with French clocks and genuine Louis XIV panelling and a painted ceiling depicting Jupiter and Juno. The Castle contains a notable collection of paintings, though many were lost in the fire, including no fewer than 36 by Joshua Reynolds. Among those to be seen today are portraits by Reynolds, three rural scenes by Gainsborough,. a range of family portraits and best known, a portrait of Henry VIII attributed to Holbein. The house is open to the public from April to October, for the most part daily except Mondays.

BRAUNSTONE HALL

Braunstone Hall, like Belgrave Hall now embedded in Leicester, was in the country when it was built for the Winstanley family in 1776. Set on rising ground in its parkland, it is a brick mansion with stone dressings. Two-and-a-half storeys high, it is topped by a cornice and a hipped roof. The house is five bays wide, with the middle bay framed by a large blank arch and with an elaborate doorway. The Braunstone estate was sold by the Winstanley family to the Borough of Leicester in 1925, mainly for housing. However, nearly 168 acres were set aside for use as a public park in which the house stands. Until recently used as a junior school, it is presently standing empty.

BROOKSBY HALL

Situated in the Wreake Valley just off the Melton Mowbray road, nine miles north-east of Leicester, Brooksby Hall, like many country houses in the two counties, has had a varied architectural history which is reflected in its appearance today. The original house seems to have dated from the late sixteenth or early seventeenth century when it was

44. *Braunstone Hall was built in 1766 for the Winstanley family. A brick mansion with stone dressings, its entrance front contains an elaborate doorway.*

the seat of the Villiers family and the birthplace of George Villiers, later created Duke of Buckingham. The family baronetcy became extinct in 1711 when the estate was bought by Sir Nathan Wright, Lord Keeper. Through much of the nineteenth century it was used as a hunting box and then, in 1911, it was purchased by Admiral Beatty of First World War fame. Finally, in 1945 Leicestershire and Rutland County Councils acquired it for use as an agricultural college which opened six years later and which it still is today.

Of the late sixteenth-early seventeenth century house, the west wing and the northern half of the east wing remain. Although altered in the early eighteenth century, only the sash windows are left of this time. In the early nineteenth century, a two-storey gabled projection was added to the west wing and then, in 1890-91, the southern half of the east wing was replaced and extended and most of the interior remodelled. Finally, other minor alterations were made by Sir Edwin Lutyens for Admiral Beatty in about 1912. The house is built on an H-plan of squared ironstone with limestone dressings and with a Swithland slate roof. It consists of two storeys and an attic, with a range of seven windows made up of a three-bay hall range between projecting wings The central bay is probably early nineteenth century, the west wing to the left has a large canted stone bay window of about 1890, and the east wing to the right ,of 1891, is similar but without the bay. Inside, there is a hall-cum-dining room designed by Lutyens and a room south-east of the hall containing panelling which is said to have come from Admiral Beatty's flagship. In the grounds are a series of plain brick student residences erected in 1956 and in 1970-72 and a pergola by the lake attributed to Lutyens. The College holds occasional open days to which the public are invited.

<u>Source:</u> John R. Hubbard, *Brooksby*, British Agricultural Colleges, 1977.

45. *Brooksby Hall, now the County of Leicestershire Agricultural College, has had a complicated architectural history. Consisting of two storeys and an attic, parts of it date from the late sixteenth century, though the exterior is largely of the late nineteenth century.*

CARLTON CURLIEU HALL

Situated on the marlstone escarpment some ten miles south-east of Leicester, Carlton Curlieu Hall dates mainly from the early seventeenth century when it was built by Sir John Bale who inherited the estate in 1621 and the north front is dated 1636. It was bought in 1664 by Sir Geoffrey Palmer, Attorney-General to Charles II, who was twice imprisoned in the Tower of London during the Commonwealth and was knighted at the Restoration. He remodelled the west front at some time before his death in 1670 and there was a second, smaller, remodelling by another Palmer in about 1820. The Palmers lived here for centuries. Despite these remodellings, the house today looks very much of a piece; moderate in size and well-maintained, it is typical of the period in which it was built. The west entrance front, two-and-a-half storeys high and with a basement, is

46. The five-gabled entrance front of Carlton Curlieu Hall dates from the early seventeenth century.

of ashlar, large blocks of wrought masonry, and comprises seven bays and five striking Dutch gables with semi-circular finials. It has a two-storey porch with an entrance arch flanked by Tuscan columns, added in the 1670s in a style which Pevsner calls conservative Jacobean. The south side of the house has three shaped gables and windows, while the north side is of ironstone.

COLD OVERTON HALL

High up in east Leicestershire, close to the Rutland border, the estate was acquired by John St John in about 1620 and it was he who built the Hall, either during the Commonwealth or shortly before his death in 1664 in a style that is transitional between early seventeenth-century classical and

that which is characteristic of the later seventeenth century. It is doubtless for that reason that Pevsner calls it "a curious mixture of archaic and advanced motifs". Small additions were made to the house in 1809 and 1828 and then, in 1914, more extensive additions were made and internal redecoration undertaken. These last additions were mostly demolished in the 1950s. What remains today, therefore, is mainly the seventeenth century house with some early nineteenth century additions. The Hall, which at the time of writing is owned by Mrs Barbara Wilson, consists of coursed and squared ironstone with limestone dressings and hipped Swithland slate roofs. It comprises three storeys with attics and consists of five bays. The west garden front has a projecting pedimented centre consisting of three bays with a two-storied flat ridged porch projecting beyond.

47. (previous page) and 48. (left) The delightful west garden front of Cold Overton Hall, a house of brick with stone dressings, which dates from the mid-seventeenth century. It contains a two-storey porch with an entrance arch flanked by Tuscan columns.

COLEORTON HALL

*L*ocated five miles east of Ashby in north-west Leicestershire, the present Hall is the third one on the site and was built between 1804 and 1808 by George Dance the Younger for Sir George Beaumont at a cost of 15,000 pounds. Beaumont, a skilled amateur painter and an important patron of the arts, had many famous friends including Coleridge, Southey, Reynolds, Wordsworth and Walter Scott, who began his novel "Ivanhoe" here. Beaumont was an art collector of note who was instrumental in helping to found the National Gallery, its nucleus being formed by the gift of his own collection.

The modestly-sized house was built by Dance in a unique combination of styles dubbed by Pevsner "stripped Gothic, Greek, and 'Hindoo'." In 1862, F. P. Cockerell added another half storey and changed the stripped down Gothic appearance of the house for a lighter, more picturesque, composition. The main front, of ashlar, consists of five bays, asymmetrical, with a projecting Tudor-style porte-cochere with a vaulted ceiling bearing on the outside the Beaumont arms and topped by the statue of a lion. On the ground and first floors are Gothic windows set in blank pointed arches. The facade is also decorated with pilaster strips and polygonal

49. *Coleorton Hall, built in the early nineteenth century, was modified some fifty years later. Its entrance front contains an impressive porte-cochere.*

turret-like buttresses on the side. The most striking feature of the interior of the building is, in the words of Frederick Whiting, "the central hall consisting of tall, narrow arches, beneath which is a circular balcony used by Sir George Beaumont for painting but described by Lady Beaumont, no doubt with good cause, as 'the Arctic Circle'."

The Hall, like the garden which is included in English Heritage's Register of Parks and Gardens of Special Historic Interest, embodies many elements of the Picturesque style which was fashionable at the turn of the nineteenth century. The garden front of the house commands a "prospect" of Bardon Hill with a series of terraces adorned with Grecian Urns.

The Winter Garden, about 100 metres south-east of the Hall, is situated in an old quarry and was designed by William Wordsworth and contains a shell grotto designed by his sister Dorothy.

Source: Frederick A. Whiting, 'A Garden Planned by Wordsworth, Coleorton Hall, Leicestershire', *Country Life,* Vol. CXXVI, 24 September 1964, pp.772-3.

DONINGTON HALL

*T*he present house is at least the third one to be built in Donington park, by Castle Donington in the north-west of the county. Its predecessors included a manor house of unknown date, possibly medieval, and a rambling hall to which an extension was added in the eighteenth century. The present Hall was built between 1790 and 1793 by William Wilkins the Elder for Francis Rawdon Hastings, the

Second Earl of Moira and first Marquess of Hastings, who was given the estate in 1789 by his uncle the Earl of Huntingdon. Situated in a hollow, the house was built in the style of Strawberry Hill Gothic, so-called from Horace Walpole's house of this name in Twickenham. Some parts of the old hall were incorporated in the new building. At the same time,

Humphry Repton, the distinguished landscape gardener, landscaped the park.

The Hastings family had first come to Donington Park at the end of the sixteenth century but, having moved into their new house at the end of the eighteenth century, they were to occupy it for little more than another hundred years, thanks largely to the profligacy of the Fourth Marquess of Hastings. Having inherited the estate from his elder brother in 1851, by the time of his death 17 years later he had gambled away most of the family fortune. The estate remained in the family 's hands for another 20 years or so but efforts to keep it proved unavailing and it was put up for sale in 1901, when it was bought by Frederick Gretton, brother of John Gretton of Stapleford Hall. He did not move into the house and at the outbreak of the First World War it was requisitioned by the Army and turned into a prisoner of war camp for German officers. At the end of the war it returned to Gretton who put it on the market in 1929 when it was bought by John Gillies Shields who had been chief steward to the Hastings

family. During the 1930s, the race track for which it has become well-known was built and extended over part of the estate. With the outbreak of the Second World War it was again taken over by the Army and the park used as a transport depot, damage being done both to the house and the park as a result of military occupation. Eventually, in 1956, Major John Gillies Shields, grandson of the owner who died in 1943, took possession of the Hall. After valiant but unavailing attempts to preserve it, he put it up for sale in 1977 when it was purchased by Sir Michael Bishop as headquarters for his British Midland Airways. Outwardly, the house is unchanged but the interior has been converted into a modern business headquarters.

The Hall, faced with white ashlar, a stone from Quarry Wood on the estate, is a rectangular two-storey building, surrounding an inner courtyard. Thirteen bays long and seven bays wide, it has a projecting chapel, four bays in width, at its north-east corner. The principal front, facing south, is dominated by a lantern tower belvedere. Although the interior was much refurbished in 1981-2, many of the original features have been retained. These include a Gothick style entrance hall with a high groined ceiling and a huge traceried rose fanlight of Georgian heraldic stained glass over the front door, the Library with its original shelves, and a Regency Drawing Room.

Sources: Anthony Squires, *Donington Park and the Hastings Connection, Kairos* Press, 1996 and John Gillies Shields, *A Brief Description of Donington Hall*, unpublished, n.d.

50. *Donington Hall, built at the end of the eighteenth century in the style of Strawberry Hill Gothic.*

GADDESBY HALL

*O*n the eastern edge of the village of Gaddesby, some eight miles north-east of Leicester, the House was originally known as Paske Hall and in the early nineteenth century belonged to John Ayre. His daughter married Colonel Cheney, a veteran of the Battle of Waterloo, and they lived in the Hall until his death in 1848 after which it passed through various hands. An agreeable house of moderate size, it dates from 1744 when it was either built or substantially rebuilt. Made of brick with limestone dressings and consisting of two stories, it had a third floor and wings, the latter being mostly added in 1868, which were demolished in 1950 when the house was remodelled by C. E. Ogden, giving it a somewhat truncated appearance. The main south-west front has a three-bay recessed centre with a central Ionic doorcase topped by a balustrade with a central crest, flanked on either side by big canted bays with stone quoins. It is set in a pleasant garden. In the beautiful church nearby is a monument to Colonel Cheney which was once in the Hall and moved in 1917. It shows him on a collapsing horse at Waterloo, where during the day's battle four horses were killed under him.

51. *The south-west front of Gaddesby Hall, built or substantially rebuilt in the mid-eighteenth century. It originally had a third storey, removed in 1950, giving the house a slightly truncated appearance.*

GOADBY MARWOOD HALL

Situated in the North Leicestershire wolds, some five miles north-east of Melton Mowbray, the original seventeenth-century house was remodelled in the mid-eighteenth century – there are rainwater heads dated 1750 – possibly by Francis Smith of Warwick. A handsome house set in a small park, it is built of coursed ironstone with Collyweston stone slate roofs in a classical Palladian style, described by Pevsner as overwhelmingly English in appearance. The south front is two-and-a-half storeys high and consists of nine bays. The centre five bays are recessed and of these the central three are under an open pediment carried on two giant Doric pilasters and contain a central projecting pedimented porch on two Roman Doric columns. To the rear, the north front is of three storeys and seven bays. A large two-storey service range was attached to the west side, also in ironstone and with Collyweston slate roofs, probably in the late nineteenth century. The interior contains a dining room with large-framed

52. *The south front of Goadby Marwood Hall. The present house was remodelled in the mid-eighteenth century in a classical Palladian style*

eighteenth-century panelling and a sitting room with earlier eighteenth-century small-framed panelling.

GRACE DIEU MANOR

Here, just to the south of the Ashby road some six miles west of Loughborough, a small priory for Augustinian canons was founded between 1235 and 1240. After its dissolution in 1539, the site was acquired by John Beaumont who converted the ruins, chiefly the chapter house and cloister, into a house and it was here that Francis Beaumont, who wrote Jacobean dramas with John Fletcher, was born. The mansion stood until 1696 when it was pulled down by Sir Ambrose Phillipps. Then, between 1833 and 1834, Ambrose Phillipps de Lisle, a noted convert to Catholicism, had a house and a nearby chapel built for him in a Tudor-Gothic style by William Railton. The house and chapel became a centre of the Catholic Revival movement of the time and here in 1837 Phillipps met Pugin , the celebrated architect of Mount St. Bernard Abbey and the designer of the interior of the Houses of Parliament. In 1841, Pugin added an extra wing to the house at Grace Dieu, altered its interior decorations, and extended the chapel. Later, in about 1900, the house was enlarged once more. After Ambrose Phillipps' death in 1883, the house was rented out and since 1933 has been a Catholic Preparatory school run by the Rosminian order. The ruins of the Priory, though in a poor condition, still stand.

Hidden behind a screen of trees on the edge of Charnwood Forest, the house faces south and east.

The main south front, which is stuccoed, has gabled wings, Perpendicular-style windows, and a central stone oriel. At the south-west end is a is a tower with a bell tower added by Pugin to join the house to the chapel. The western entrance front is also stuccoed. The chapel, which is mainly Perpendicular in style, has a separate western entrance into the nave, to which Pugin added a wide north aisle in 1848. The chapel contains a shrine to the Blessed Sacrament with an elaborate stone canopy, both designed by Pugin.

Source: Leanda de Lisle and Peter Stanford, *The Catholics and their Homes*, Harper Collins, 1995, pp.91-95.

53. *Grace Dieu Manor dates from 1833 when it was built in a Tudor-Gothic style. An extra wing was added by Pugin in 1841 and the house was enlarged again in about 1900.*

HUSBANDS BOSWORTH HALL

Standing on high ground on the southern border of the county in a small park on the east side of the village, Bosworth Hall has been a centre of Catholic influence in Leicestershire since the early seventeenth century. Purchased in 1630 by Lady Grace Fortescue, daughter of Sir John Manners of Haddon Hall, Derbyshire, it has been owned at various times by connections of the old Catholic Families of Fortescue, Turville and Talbot and eventually, in 1942, passed to Mrs Turville Constable Maxwell. It is now owned by Mrs Robert Constable Maxwell

The present Hall consists of two houses standing back to back, which are now separate dwellings. The older one dates from the medieval period of which a massive wooden cruck truss and stone walls remain. It was largely rebuilt of timber framing in the late sixteenth century and then recased in brick, probably in the later seventeenth century. It was then restored in Victorian times and today presents a range of five gables, with the outer two projecting as wings. All the wings are two-and-a-half storeys high. Between 1792 and 1793, the architect Joseph Bonomi designed a new, taller brick house with the principal front facing south-east, for the then owner Francis Fortescue Turville. However it appears that Bonomis design was not carried out and another one by the architect John Wagstaff was built right at the end of the eighteenth century. The resulting edifice is a massive three storeys high and five bays wide with a central portico with Ionic columns. Standing a few feet to the east of the older building, the new house was originally connected to it by a passage. Then, in the late nineteenth century, the facade was restyled in a Victorian Tudor fashion and a northern kitchen extension built.

Source: *Victoria County History of Leicestershire*, Vol. 5, 1964, pp.29-30.

54. *The older part of Husbands Bosworth Hall dating from medieval times was rebuilt several times in later centuries. This photograph shows its range of five gables with the outer two projecting as wings.*

INGARSBY OLD HALL

Situated to the north of the A47 six miles east of Leicester, the medieval Manor of Ingarsby belonged to Leicester Abbey, which in 1469 depopulated the village in order to enclose the land for stock-rearing. What remains in the form of grassed over streets, house sites and boundary ditches is situated to the north of the A47 six miles east of Leicester, probably the most complete deserted medieval village site in the county. After the Dissolution, the manor was bought by Brian Cave and in 1621 it was sold to Sir Robert Bannister. The manor house, adjacent to the village and surrounded on three sides by a moat,

55. *Ingarsby Old Hall consists of two houses joined together. The older one to the left of the photograph dates from the late fifteenth or early sixteenth century. That to the right is possibly seventeenth-century in origin and was subsequently altered. The two ranges were joined together by a short section in 1936.*

consists of two ranges which were originally separate. The east range may date from the late fifteenth century or may have been built by Brian Cave in the 1540s. Constructed of stone, it consists of two floors and with its mullioned windows and arched doorway is like a chapel in appearance. The west range possibly dates originally from Bannister's time but its facade has been altered. This consists of plain ashlar and comprises two storeys with a central porch , a window on either side and a steep slate roof with two dormer windows. The two ranges were joined by a short section in 1936 when the interior was also remodelled.

KEYTHORPE HALL

Situated on the A47, some 10 miles east of Leicester, Keythorpe Hall was built in a plain, late Georgian style for Lord Berners in about 1843. The main building, of yellow brick with stone quoins, is of two storeys and five bays wide. The central three bays project and have porch with Tuscan columns and a pediment. To the rear is a five-bay wing of two-and-a-half storeys, possibly earlier in date than the main wing, and to the left is a lower three-bay wing.

56. *Keythorpe Hall was built about 1843, of brick with stone quoins, in a plain late Georgian style.*

LANGTON HALL

Situated by the village of West Langton, north of Market Harborough, Langton Hall is a large three-storey building of ironstone and limestone on a shallow E-plan. It is said to have been built by Thomas Staveley in the early seventeenth century and the general layout is consistent with that date. His son, the antiquary, Thomas Staveley was born here in 1626. The house was subsequently been much altered and it is not clear how much of the original building remains. Additions were made in the 1660s from which the core of the house dates and there is a date-stone , probably not in its original position, of 1660 and a weather vane of 1669. The house was used as a hunting lodge by Hugo Meynell, Master of the Quorn Hunt, in the 1770s. The principal front which faces east was Gothicised in

1802 by the then owner, the Reverend James Ord, and given a crenellated parapet, a projecting porch and a tall tower. Further alterations were made in the early part of this century. Externally, the north wing appears to be the oldest part of the house with its stone-mullioned windows. Internally, the entrance hall is panelled with cedar and the walls of the large and small drawing rooms are covered with late eighteenth century Venetian lace. On the north side of the house is an eighteenth century brick stable range.

For various periods, from the mid-eighteenth century to the end of the nineteenth century, the Hall was leased out, chiefly as a hunting box. At the time of writing, the Hall is being restored and converted into five units. In the park, which lies on the north side of the road to Kibworth Beauchamp, are avenues of trees radiating from the south and east fronts of the house.

57. *Langton Hall was built in the early seventeenth century and its principal front, shown here, was 'Gothicised' in 1802. At the time this picture was taken (Summer 1988), it was being converted into five units.*

Source: *Victoria County History of Leicestershire*, Vol. 5, 1964, p.195.

LAUNDE ABBEY

*L*ying in the green valley of the River Chater by the Rutland border, Launde was founded between 1119 and 1125 not as an abbey but as a priory for Augustinian or Black Canons, by Richard Bassett and his wife Maud. After the Dissolution it went to Thomas Cromwell who did not survive long thereafter and it soon passed to his son Gregory; between them the Cromwells built a house on the site. In 1603 the estate passed to Sir William Smith and thereafter to the Clark, Halford and Finch families until, in 1765, it was bought by John Simpson of Leicester who became High Sheriff of the county in 1775. Simpson enlarged the house and then in about 1840 it was restored and considerably enlarged by the Dawson family of Long Whatton who had acquired the estate by marriage. The Dawsons remained here for over 100 years, when the estate came to Cecil Rawlins Coleman and his wife Lilian,

58. *Launde Abbey which dates from the mid-sixteenth century was restored and considerably enlarged in about 1840.*

who in December 1957 presented it to the Diocese of Leicester as a Church Conference Centre and Retreat.

Of the original house built by the Cromwells to an H-shape, the mullioned and transomed windows remain. According to Pevsner, the present house looks early seventeenth century in style which perhaps suggests it was rebuilt by its owner at that time. However, it was certainly enlarged by Simpson in the latter part of the eighteenth century and further altered in 1844. The house, which faces west, remains an H-plan with the north wing on the site of the nave of the priory church. It has a gabled five-bay centre with gabled projecting wings. Inside, north of the entrance hall is the main staircase dating from the eighteenth century, while in the dining room is a fireplace dated 1689 and a section of panelling dated 1663 and 1676. Above the dining room is a smaller room known as Cromwell's closet dating from Cromwell's time and containing the remains of a possibly medieval garde-robe.

All that remains visible of the Priory is the chapel which lies to the east of the house. Originally the chancel of the priory church, it seems to date from about 1125 and was remodelled first in the early or mid-thirteenth century and later in Perpendicular style. It was much restored by Railton, architect of Grace Dieu Manor, in 1840-41. Of particular interest are the east and south windows which contain much late medieval glass and the monument to Gregory Cromwell which Pevsner considers to be one of the purest early Renaissance monuments in England.

Source: Philip E. Hunt, *Launde Abbey*, Launde Abbey, Second Edition, 1982; and Heather E. Broughton, *Family and Estate Records in the Leicestershire Records Office*, Leicester Museums, Arts and Records Service, 1991.

LOCKINGTON HALL

*T*he Bainbrigge family built the original house here, two miles north-west of Kegworth on the Derbyshire border, in about 1688. It subsequently came to the Reverend Philip Storey who remodelled it between 1797 and 1804. Then, in about 1872, Nathaniel Charles Curzon, related to the Curzons of Kedleston in Derbyshire, moved his family seat here and rebuilt the house, adding the two west wings and the large porch. During the last war, the house was used as a maternity home. The Hall today is owned by Charles Coaker, whose father married a Curzon, and for the past 24 years he has leased it to an architectural firm. The late seventeenth century house was of stone and originally consisted of two storeys with a hipped roof with dormers and a central cupola. The remodelling at the end of the eighteenth century added an attic

storey and a Tuscan colonnade between the wings. The 1872 alterations effectively doubled the size of the house by adding two-storey brick service wings. At the same time, a portico was added to the north front and square bay windows to the south. The interior contains a late seventeenth-century staircase in the upper storey of the south wing and the large main staircase was inserted in the late nineteenth century in a late seventeenth-century style.

59. *(above) and* **60.** *(left). Lockington Hall was built in the early seventeenth century, extensively remodelled at the end of the eighteenth century and doubled in size in 1872. The first photograph shows the garden front with the older part of the house to the right and the late nineteenth-century service wings to the left. The second photograph shows the entrance front with its portico.*

LOWESBY HALL

*T*here was an earlier house here, some nine miles east-north-east of Leicester, of Ketton stone, probably dating from the seventeenth century. This forms the core of the present house which was probably built by Isaac Wollaston in about 1707. In 1772 the heiress to the Wollastons married Thomas Fowke and the Hall remained in the possession of the Fowkes, generations of whom are buried in the nearby church, right into the present century. The present owners are Mr and Mrs David Wilson.

The large attractive house, of red brick with blue headers, is of two storeys with attics and a hipped Swithland slate roof. The entrance front consists of nine bays, with typical projecting wings and a central doorcase with a swan-necked pediment. Above the central section is a pediment with a shield of the arms of the Fowke family. The garden front is of eleven bays with the central three pedimented and projecting and also containing a doorcase with a swan-necked pediment. To the right, or east, of the garden front is a lower two-storey wing which was slightly lengthened in 1910 by Sir Edwin Lutyens for

Captain Harold Brassey who had rented the house from the Fowkes. Lutyens and Gertrude Jekyll at this time laid out the garden with a terrace and a semi-circular set of terrace steps. In 1910, Lutyens also built the brick stables in an eighteenth century fashion. The interior of the house contains a principal room decorated in the style of the early eighteenth century with panelling, and classical doorcases and fireplace. In the parkland, about 400 metres north-west of the Hall, is the site of a deserted village.

61. (above) and 62. (left). The first photograph is of the entrance front to the early eighteenth-century Lowesby Hall with its projecting wings, doorcase with swan-necked pediment, and pediment above with its coat of arms. The second photograph shows the garden front, eleven bays wide, with the projecting central section three bays wide. Leading up to it are the garden terrace and the semi-circular set of steps laid out by Gertrude Jekyll and Sir Edwin Lutyens in 1910.

MARKET BOSWORTH HALL

For centuries the Dixie family dominated the small town of Market Bosworth in south-west Leicestershire. The first member of the family to come here, Sir Wolstan Dixie, who made his fortune in the fur trade and was made Lord Mayor of London in 1585, purchased the estate with its timbered hall in about 1593. Here the family remained until 1885 when Beaumont Dixie sold the estate and house to Charles Tollemache Scott. In 1958 Beaumont's grandson, Alexander Archibald Douglas Wolstan, returned here and after his death in 1975 the house became first a hospital and now a hotel. The house was probably built by Sir Beaumont Dixie, who demolished the old manor house, in the 1680s or 1690s, was altered between 1837 and 1850 and, again, by Tollemache Scott in 1885.

The mansion is essentially a fine Baroque house in red brick with ashlar dressings throughout. The low pitched slated hipped roofs probably date from the middle of the nineteenth century. The entrance, front is raised on a terrace with stone balustrades and a central flight of stairs. It comprises nine bays, with the central three projecting under a pediment on elegant fluted pilasters with a shield of arms of Sir Beaumont Dixie who built the house in the gable. The principal angles are also marked by stone fluted pilasters. The south elevation is also raised on a terrace and consists of eleven bays with the central three topped by a pediment with another shield of arms in the gable. Internally, most of the decoration and fittings date from the major alterations of 1885,

though some of the late seventeenth-century features are still visible, including a fine staircase. In the cellar are three iron gates removed from Newgate Prison cells in 1903. To the south of the house is the fine park, now a Leicestershire Country Park, with many trees planted by Tollemache Scott.

63. *The central section of the west front of Market Bosworth Hall with its elegant fluted pilasters and pediment with a shield of arms.*

NEVILL HOLT HALL

The mansion stands on high ground overlooking the Welland vally in the extreme south-east of the county. During the Middle Ages much of the land here was owned by Thomas Palmer who by 1444 had acquired it all. When, having no son, he died in 1474, the estate went to his daughter, Katherine. She had married William Nevill of Rolleston in Nottinghamshire, so that the estate came to the Nevills. They appended their name to the place and here they stayed until 1868 when the whole estate was sold by auction. It was eventually bought, in 1876, by Edward Cunard of the famous shipping business. When he died suddenly, a year later, the estate passed to his brother, Sir Bache Cunard, who with increasing difficulty maintained the Hall until 1912. The estate came on the market in 1918 when it was split up and in 1919 the buildings and some land were purchased by the Reverend C. A. Bowlker, at that time head of the Lower School at Uppingham, for use as a preparatory school, which it remains today.

The Hall itself is a building of many periods and having grown together with the church, which contains a chapel and various monuments to the

64. *This panorama of Nevill Holt Hall shows a building of many periods together with a church.*

Nevills, provides an imposing spectacle. The core of the house is the stone-built Great Hall which dates from the fourteenth century with a late fourteenth century roof and a fifteenth century porch and bay window probably added by Thomas Palmer and his Nevill son-in-law. The latter two are of particular architectural interest. The porch is two-storied and contains Thomas Palmer's coat of arms, a fleur de lys, and that of his second wife above the windows; and the bay, which also consists of two storeys, has buttresses at each angle carrying beasts and, above them, wild men. Between 1591 and 1632, the Nevills extended the Hall and further additions were made between 1672 and 1728. The facade was Gothicised about 1830, a process which was completed by Sir Bache Cunard after 1876 when he rebuilt the whole front to the east of the porch. The stable block was probably built in the 1660s or 1670s. The house and chapel are occasionally open to the public.

Source: A detailed unpublished account of the Nevill family and the Hall by Roger Willson who also wrote the Visitor's Guide to the Church and the Hall.

NOSELEY HALL

Situated in attractive wooded country south-east of Leicester, the Hall and its private chapel remain, the village which stood to the north-west of the present park having been depopulated in the sixteenth century. Thomas Hesilrige acquired the estate through marriage at the end of the fourteenth century. The family retained the surname until 1818, when Sir Arthur Grey Hesilrige, the eleventh baronet, changed it to Hazlerigg and so it has remained. There was a medieval manor house here but no trace of it survives. The present house was completely rebuilt in the early eighteenth century by Sir Robert Hesilrige who died in 1721 and rainwater heads dated 1723 suggest the building was completed

65. *The bay window at Nevill Holt Hall dating from the fifteenth century.*

after his death by his widow Dorothy. Noseley Hall, the home of Lord Hazlerigg, is a large two-storey brick building, with attics, a balustraded parapet and hipped slate roofs. However, most of it was

66. *The principal south front of Noseley Hall, eleven bays wide, with its projecting centre containing a doorcase, and its balustraded parapet.*

occupied by the saloon which Pevsner describes "as a wonderful surprise", having fine Baroque decoration and Rococo motifs, dating from the 1730s and 1740s. These include heavy Corinthian pilasters which support a large cornice above which are shorter pilasters topped by a shell motif. Another room of considerable interest is the former dining room with its Rococo decoration. The chapel to the house dates mainly from the thirteenth century. In the Autumn of 1998 the great majority of the contents of the house were sold, and the house itself is likely to be converted into a conference centre, in which the present Lord Hazlerigg will continue to live.

cement-rendered in the late nineteenth century, though the original brick can be seen at the back of the house. The principal front, facing south, is eleven bays wide with the three central bays set forward, containing a central doorcase. On either side are bays with balustrading above. This central section is

OSBASTON HALL

Situated near Market Bosworth, there was an earlier house here which has been incorporated into the present one which outwardly appears a wholly eighteenth century building. Nichols (1811) says of it "The mansion is of brick and stone, rather low but not inelegant". The house, owned by the de Lisles, consists of three ranges round a courtyard, the fourth side being spanned by a twentieth-century wing. The two-storey east range (shown right) seems to date from the early eighteenth century and consists of eleven bays with stone pilasters in pairs at either end. The south entrance front, which has a

rainwater head dated 1750, has a three-bay recessed centre which is flanked on either side by two bays. Both the west and the south ranges contain evidence of the earlier house. Inside the house is a seventeenth-century staircase which presumably came from the earlier building, while the east range has the more elaborate interior, almost all of which dates from the early eighteenth century. There is a large walled kitchen garden, which is now managed organically, and has a number of open days throughout the year.

67. (overleaf) and 68. (above). The first photograph shows the early eight-eenth-century east wing of Osbaston Hall, eleven bays wide with pairs of stone pilasters at either end. The second shows the entrance front which dates from the mid-eighteenth century.

PEATLING PARVA HALL

Peatling Parva Hall, lying in attractive upland country some 8 miles south of Leicester, has had a complicated architectural history. It began life as an early eighteenth century Queen Anne three-storied L-shaped farmhouse, which today is the altered west wing of the house. Later in the century, a south wing of the same height, but consisting only of two stories, and a canted east end were added. For some time from about 1910 the house and estate were in the ownership of the Gemmill family who made their fortune from armaments and between 1913 and 1914 they had the house, in Pevsner's words, "almost

69. The garden front of Peatling Parva Hall, a house dating from the early eighteenth century, very largely remodelled early this century.

entirely manufactured" in a handsome Queen Anne style by Blow and Billerey. Various other changes were made at this time including moving the entrance front from the east to the south wing. Blow also almost entirely refitted the interior. Today, the compact house of red brick with stone quoins, is attractively set in a small park. The south entrance front is of five bays and two storeys, the left-hand bay an addition by Blow who also added the full height porch. The garden front is also of five bays, the outer bays being canted with bay windows on each floor. The house is owned by Mr and Mrs Ian McAlpine.

PRESTWOLD HALL

*T*he Packes came to Prestwold, three miles north-east of Loughborough, in about 1654 when Christopher Packe, who became Mayor of London and was knighted by Cromwell, acquired the

70. *The garden front of Prestwold Hall which was comprehensively remodelled in the 1840s in a classical Italianate style.*

estate from its then owner, Sir Harry Skipwith. The Hall is still occupied by the family in the shape of its present head, Mr S. J. Packe-Drury-Lowe. There was probably a Jacobean house here which was incorporated into another built about 1780 for Charles James Packe. It was of brick and had three storeys and seven bays. Then, in 1805, the architect William Wilkins the elder added a dining room to the east side of the house, employing what Pevsner calls the purer form of the Greek Revival style. Finally, between 1842 and 1844, the house was comprehensively remodelled by William Burn for Charles William Packe in an elegant classical Italianate style and all that is now visible is his work. Hussey writes of it that Burn's treatment of the house was remarkable, transforming it into something more akin to the Reform Club in London than to the popular idea of an early Victorian mansion. Indeed, in this respect, it provides a complete contrast with, for example, Beaumanor Park which is of approximately the same date.

The earlier brick house has been replaced and extended using Ancaster stone to reface the west and south fronts. The west entrance front is of three storeys and comprises nine bays, with the three central ones recessed. In the centre is a projecting porte-cochere with four Doric columns. The south garden front is also of three storeys but consists of eleven bays, while the eastern front, a completely new addition by Burn, comprises one bay of ashlar and four of painted brickwork Pevsner describes the interior as "most impressive and distinctly Italianate", the finest room being the entrance hall with its richly coloured marble walls and painted coffered ceiling, below which are busts of poets from Chaucer to Scott. The parkland and gardens are Grade II listed of special interest.

Source: Christopher Hussey, "Prestwold Hall, Leicestershire, Seat of Lt. Col. and Mrs Packe-Drury-Lowe", *Country Life, Vol. 16*, 1959, pp.828-831.

QUENBY HALL

Quenby Hall lies some eight miles east of Leicester. The Ashby family owned the estate from the thirteenth century until 1904 and Quenby Hall, described by Pevsner as "the most important early seventeenth century house in the county", was built for George Ashby at that time: the clock on the building is dated 1620, the rainwater heads 1621, and the

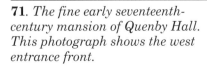

71. *The fine early seventeenth-century mansion of Quenby Hall. This photograph shows the west entrance front.*

inscription over the porch 1630. Shuckburgh Ashby, who had built the fine brick cottages in the nearby village of Hungarton, acquired the Hall in 1759 when it was in poor condition and made major structural alterations and modernised the interior in about 1769. The interior was again reinstated in a Jacobean style by Bodley between 1905 and 1907, and again by J. A. Gotch until about 1913. Throughout these changes, the exterior remained virtually unchanged, the house being built on a conventional H-plan in a late Tudor style, so that it is rather old-fashioned for its period. The entrance front is on the west and is of red brick diapered with blue brick, with stone plinths, quoins and dressings. The mansion is of three storeys, with a canted bay at either end, flanked by recessed bays and in the centre a projecting porch. The east front has only one canted bay which contains the doorway. The parkland is included in the English Heritage Register of Parks and Gardens of Special Interest. The site of the medieval village of Quenby, depopulated in the late fifteenth century is in the park some 300 metres south of the Hall. The mansion is now owned by The Squire de Lisle, formerly of Garendon Hall, who has meticulously maintained the fabric.

QUORN HALL

*T*he Farnham family, who until relatively recently were resident in Quorn House, their main seat, on the west side of the village, had an unbroken connection with Quorn which went back to about 1284. Quorn Hall, on the east side of the village, originally known as the Nether Hall in contrast to Quorn House known as the Over Hall, was the seat of a junior branch of the Farnham family from the mid-fifteenth century onwards. The house was bought in 1753 by Hugo Meynell, Master of the Quorn Hunt and "the Father of English Fox Hunting". In about 1755 he built new stables and kennels to the north-west of the house, traces of which remain, and in about 1790 he added an extra storey and more reception rooms to the Hall. The south front, facing the River Soar, retains its original H-plan and consists of three storeys with a pedimented three-bay centre and two-bay wings on either side toped by hipped roofs. The north front is composed of fifteenth century brick with a pedimented centre. The Hall continued as the official

72. *The south front of Quorn Hall with its pedimented three-bay centre and wings on either side.*

residence on the Master of the Quorn Hunt, passing through various hands, until the Hunt moved out of the stables in 1906. In 1855, Edward Warner took up residence here and it was he who had planted the beautiful avenue of chestnut trees leading from the Hall in the direction of Barrow-upon-Soar, now partly cut through by the A6 by-pass. In 1929, after the death of Captain Warner, the family left the district and the house became the home of the Quorn Country Club. In 1937 it was bought by Leicestershire County Council as a hall of residence for students of Loughborough College. During the war it was taken over by the Admiralty to house naval personnel undertaking courses, being handed back to Loughborough College once the war was over. Since 1977 it has been an International Education Centre, accommodating parties of foreign students on educational visits.

Sources: Donald H.C. Wix et al., *Bygone Quorn in Pictures*, Rawlins Community College, n.d.; and an unpublished account of Quorn Hall supplied by the International Education Centre.

QUORN HOUSE

*J*ust when the first house was built here, on the west side of the village of Quorn, it is impossible to say. However, the home of the Farnhams for centuries, it appears to have been pulled down in 1747. Then, in 1820, the family built the present house in a plain Regency style. Some additions were made to the house in about 1860 in a style similar to the original, and again in 1900, some of which were demolished in 1905 and 1955. The house is of red brick, two storeys high, and its principal west front faces the attractive parkland in which it is set. It contains gently curving bows, typical of the Regency period: one at the north end, flanked by three bays, then the second one, and finally another three bays It is capped by a stone parapet with balustrades. The south front is much narrower, consisting of two shallow bows with a bay between. Inside, are an original cantilever stone staircase with wrought iron balustrades and interiors dating mainly from about 1880 in an Elizabethan style. The Farnhams moved out a few years ago and the house is presently occupied by Rosemary Conley's Diet and Fitness Clubs Training Centre.

Source: Donald H.C. Wix et al., *Ibid.*

73. *The west front of Quorn House built for the Farnham family in 1820 in a plain Regency style.*

ROTHLEY HALL

The manor of Rothley, five miles south-east of Loughborough, was granted to the Holy Order of the Knights Templar by Henry II early in the thirteenth century and they built a chapel there which still stands and is open to visitors. In 1312, the Templars Order was suppressed by the Pope and the lands transferred to the Knights Hospitallers who held it until 1540. The manor was acquired by the Babington family in 1565 and they had their home here until 1846. Thomas Babington Macaulay, the distinguished historian and literary writer, was born here. After 1846, the Hall passed through various private hands until 1960 when it was turned into Rothley Court Hotel.

The Hall today is the north wing of an H-shaped house. Some medieval fragments remain but essentially it dates from the late sixteenth or early seventeenth century and consists of a five-bay centre and three-bay wings. Some remodelling took place in the eighteenth century and the south gable and chimney are dated 1742. Then, in 1894-5, alterations were made in an Elizabethan style, including the entrance front, a Tuscan-style gallery and a big bay window. Inside, the fittings are all, in Pevsner's words, "heavy Jacobean woodwork of 1894-5". Beyond the house stretches an eighteenth century landscaped park.

74. *The entrance front to Rothley Hall, dating from the late sixteenth or seventeenth century and substantially remodelled at the end of the nineteenth century. To the right is the mid-thirteenth century chapel.*

SCRAPTOFT HALL

*T*he Wigley family originated in Derbyshire and seem to have formed their first connections with Scraptoft, which stands on rising ground on the east side of Leicester, in the early sixteenth century. There was an early seventeenth century manor house on the site which according to Nichols was built or considerably enlarged by Letitia, wife of Sir Edward Wigley, in about 1730. The Hall carries the date 1723 on the rainwater heads of the rear elevation. The Hall and estate remained with the Wigley family until 1765 when it passed to the Hartopps who remained lords of the manor until they disposed of the estate after the First World War. In 1954, the Hall was bought by Leicester City Council for the City of Leicester College of Education and new student accommodation and other rooms were subsequently built in the grounds. Today, the site is a campus of de Montfort University.

The house was rebuilt in the early eighteenth century to a square plan and is of three storeys and has a basement. The main west front is of five bays, faced with ashlar, topped by a parapet which curves up at both ends and in the middle. The central bay is flanked by Corinthian pilasters and the main doorway, approached by a flight of stone steps, is topped by a pediment with a keystone bearing the Wigley monogram. The east, garden, front is similar to the west one and to the right is a one-storey wing added in 1869. Inside are a black and white marble floor in the entrance hall, an oak staircase, probably early eighteenth century in date, and seventeenth century stone fireplaces from the earlier house. To the north-east of the mansion are the coach house and stables, dating from 1733, of brick with Swithland slate roofs. Of particular interest is the very fine wrought-iron screen and gates of about 1725 which stand between the west forecourt and the road.

Source: *Victoria County History of Leicestershire*, Vol. 5, 1964, pp.228-9.

75. *(above)* and **76.** *(right). The first photograph is of the main west front of Scraptoft Hall dating from the early eighteenth century. The second shows the fine screen and gates of about 1725, at the end of the entrance drive.*

SHENTON HALL

The Wollaston family have lived at Shenton, near Market Bosworth, for centuries, as indeed they still do. The original house seems to have been built by William Wollaston in 1629 in a restrained English style typical of the period, and was altered in 1800 and again in about 1862. The house, of dark red brick with stone dressings, consists of two storeys. The north-west front dates from the time of the first building, while the south-east side was "considerably improved" and given projecting wings in about 1800. The 1862 additions, which included the fitting in of the space between the two and new rooms at the south-west end, substantially altered the character of the house by giving it what Pevsner describes as a "romantic distinctly Victorian silhouette" when seen from the south-west. There is also a gatehouse, dating from 1629, which like the house is of dark red brick and with stone dressings, and to the west of the house a fine 1709 dovecote.

77. *The early seventeenth-century brick gatehouse of Shenton Hall. Beyond it is the house dating originally from the early seventeenth century and much altered in the nineteenth century.*

SKEFFINGTON HALL

Skeffington Hall lies by the village some ten miles east of Leicester on the south side of the A47. The Skeffington family first came here in the twelfth century and between 1450 and 1460, Thomas Skeffington built a house here. Then in the sixteenth century Sir William Skeffington, Lord Deputy of Ireland built a grand house,

78. *To the left of the photograph is the south wing of Skeffington Hall with its early sixteenth-century bay window, and to the right is the front east wing, dating mainly from the seventeenth century.*

presumably replacing or incorporating parts of the earlier house. In 1860, the estate was bought by William Tailby, founder of the Billesdon Hunt, and Tailbys lived here until the 1930s. Pevsner describes the present mansion as an "archaeological puzzle", in that it contains elements dating variously from the late fifteenth century, the early sixteenth century, several dates in the seventeenth century, and the early eighteenth century. In addition, major alterations occurred in about 1810 and again between 1843 and 1850, and minor alterations in about 1870. The front east range is mainly of the seventeenth century and gables were added about 1800. It contains a stone doorcase dating from the early eighteenth century. The south wing is the earliest part of the house and contains a spectacular ashlar-faced early sixteenth-century bay window.

STANFORD HALL

The Caves have lived in Stanford, right on the Northamptonshire border by the River Avon, since the fifteenth century and, in 1540, after the Dissolution of the Monasteries, Thomas Cave purchased the manor. In 1697, Sir Roger Cave, the second baronet, commissioned William Smith of Warwick to demolish the old manor house which stood on the Northamptonshire side of the river and build a new one on the Leicestershire side. In the early eighteenth century, Sir Thomas Cave married Margaret Verney who brought the ancient Irish Barony of Braye into the family, albeit terminated. However, the Barony was restored in 1839 in favour of Sarah Otway-Cave who became the third Baroness and her descendant, Lady Braye, is the present owner of the house.

79. *The fine classical house of Stanford Hall, built between 1697 and 1703 and added to in about 1735. To the right of the photograph is the south front dating* from *the earlier period.*

The mansion is built of ashlar and is described by Pevsner as the finest of its date in the county. Begun in 1697, it was still incomplete when William Smith died in 1703, by which time he had designed the south front in a conservative, classical, late seventeenth century style. It consists of nine bays, with the centre five bays slightly recessed, and with a slate roof with dormer windows. The east front was added about 1735 by Smith's brother, Francis, and it too consists of seven bays, but all on a level, with triangular stone pediments over all the windows. The west and north fronts, also dating from this period, are quite plain. Inside, the public entrance by the east door leads to the main cantilevered staircase of about 1730. The ballroom, created in 1745 by William Smith the younger, has a ceiling covered with Rococo decoration at the corners and a heavily moulded cornice. The east front looks towards the brick stables built by Francis Smith in 1737 and an essential part of Stanford's attractiveness. The house and stables are set in a beautiful parkland with a fine late seventeenth century northern double avenue of trees and much mid-eighteenth century landscaping. The park is included in the Register of Parks and Gardens of Special Historic Interest. The house and park are open to the public mainly at weekends from Easter to the end of September.

STAPLEFORD PARK

Here, about five miles east of Melton Mowbray, stand the Hall and church set in a large park. The village that was once here was depopulated about 1500. Stapleford, pronounced 'Stappleford', was the main seat of the Sherard family who acquired it from the Earl of Lancaster in 1402. About 1502, Thomas Sherard built a house which was "repayred" in 1633 by his grandson William who had been knighted in 1622 and given the Irish Barony of Leitrim five years later. Between 1670 and 1680, the second Baron added a second house, which was remodelled between 1768 and 1769 by the family who in 1718 had become Earls of Harborough. The last of the Sherards, Robert, sixth Earl of Harborough, died in 1859 and his widow in 1886. The estate was sold and eventually purchased in 1894 by John Gretton who oversaw much alteration and new building. In 1899 he was succeeded by his son who subsequently became Lord Gretton. In both World Wars the mansion became a convalescent hospital for wounded soldiers. In 1986, the house and estate were sold to John Payton, the American businessman, who later died in a car crash, and converted into a hotel, as it is today.

Given its varied history, Stapleford Park reflects various building periods. The earliest part of the house, known as Lady Abigail's Range after Lady Sherard, is on the east side of the house. Originally built and dated 1500, it was "recomposed" by Lord Sherard in 1633 and under the eaves bears the inscription "William Lord Sherard of Letrym repayred this Buylding Anno Domini 1633". The picturesque composition, described by Pevsner as "reminiscent of Flemish town halls and quite unimaginable in its Tudor state", is of three bays with two storeys and above the second storey are three cross-eaves dormer windows with crocketed gables above. Between the windows on the first floor are twelve niches containing statues, the six to the right dating from about 1500 and the six to the left from 1633. The latter were added by Lady Abigail and are supposedly Sherard ancestors – including no less a personage than William the Conqueror – named in banners below them.

80. *The earlier part of Stapleford Park is to the right of the photograph, being built in 1500 and recomposed in 1633. To the left is the late seventeenth-century house,now a hotel.*

By contrast, the two-storey late seventeenth-century house is relatively restrained. The north front is of seven bays with the eaves raised slightly over the middle window, and the east front with nine-by-one bays projects slightly north. The symmetrical west front is of seven bays, and the south front, dating from the late nineteenth century, has a projecting balustraded seven-bay centre, to which at the time it was built a northern service wing was added. The interior of the house contains some late seventeenth-century fittings and decorations. The stone Jacobean-style stables, some distance from the house, were built in 1899 and are praised by Pevsner as being "probably the finest in this hunting county". The house and stables are set in a fine park, landscaped by Capability Brown in 1775 and included in the English Heritage Register of Parks and Gardens of Special Historic Interest.

STAUNTON HAROLD HALL

*O*ne cannot do better than quote Pevsner's opening sentence under this entry, "For position, Staunton Harold, the house and chapel, are unsurpassed in the county – certainly as far as Englishness is concerned." The Shirleys, who took their name from one of their manors in Derbyshire, began their connection with Staunton Harold, which lies three miles north east of Ashby, in 1423, when Ralph Shirley married Margaret, the heiress of John de Staunton whose family had held Staunton Harold since the twelfth century. In the latter part of the seventeenth century, Sir Robert Shirley became the first Earl Ferrers and the Ferrers made additions and alterations to the existing hall in the early 1700s and again, more extensively, in the 1760s. The Ferrers family remained here until 1955 when the house was sold for demolition. Happily, it was saved at the last moment when it was purchased by Leonard Cheshire as a home for terminally ill patients. Today, it is the Sue Ryder Specialist Palliative Care Home.

The Shirleys built themselves a house here, perhaps soon after arriving in the fifteenth century, and fragments of the original house are embedded in the present building. The first Earl Ferrers added a north range at some time after 1669, which was replaced by the present one in about 1700. It consists of five bays with a central doorway with a segmental pediment on Ionic half-columns and a balustraded parapet. The rest of the house, of brick with stone dressings, was erected for the fifth Earl Ferrers in

81. *The fine mid-seventeenth century chapel at Staunton Harold is in the foreground, and behind it is the east front of the Hall.*

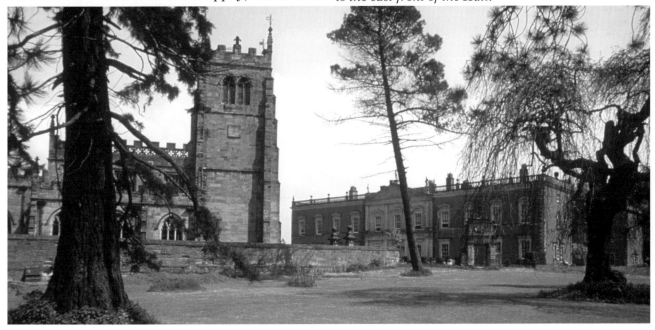

1763. The principal, east, front is of two storeys with a three-bay ashlar-pedimented centrepiece. The south front, known as the Lion Court from the leaded lion perched above the parapet, is of two-and-a-half storeys with projecting wings, all in bright red brick. The interior of the Hall reveals something of the earlier building, including the Justice Room, dating from the seventeenth century now restored to its original use as a chapel and with original panelling. The saloon on the first floor also dates from this period with its Venetian-style paintings set in ovals and its plasterwork ceiling with eagles carrying garlands. The staircase hall, inserted into the building by the fifth Earl in about 1764, consists of three cantilevered stone flights with a fine wrought-iron balustrade. Perhaps the best work is in the library, of the same date, a long room on the ground floor of the north wing with its pedimented bookcases and plaster cornices. To the northwest of the house is the stable block now used as a craft centre.

But Staunton Harold should be seen not only for the house and stables but also for the fine chapel now in the care of the National Trust. It is probably unique in being perhaps the only complete survival of a church built during the Commonwealth. With its moving inscription over the west entrance and its remarkably complete contemporary fittings, it is one of the most rewarding buildings in the county. Also of great interest are the splendid gatepiers, known as the Golden Gates, which mark the approach to the house from the north-east with their barley sugar columns and pediments surmounted by the Shirley hound and stag. The parkland setting of the house and chapel, included in the English Heritage Register of Parks and Gardens of Special Historic Interest, is equally fine with its valley with streams and lakes running through the estate to the east of the Hall. It was "naturalised" in the latter part of the eighteenth century. The stables which have been converted into a craft centre are open daily to the public and the chapel may be seen at stated times.

STRETTON HALL

Stretton Hall, which lies just off the A6, five miles south-east of Leicester, was probably built between1670 and 1690 for George Hewett. Of reddish-purple brick with stone architraves to the windows, it is two stories high with attic windows in the gable ends. Substantial additions were made at the end of the last century including bay windows on the east front, which also has a fine pediment containing a coat of arms dating back to the original building. The house became a hospital in the inter-war years and remained so until about 1970. After lying unoccupied for many years, it is presently (Autumn 1998) being restored and converted into units and houses are to be built on the estate.

82. *Stretton Hall, now being converted into units, dates originally from the early seventeenth century.*

SWITHLAND HALL

*T*he Danvers family, later Earls of Lanesborough, lived at Swithland, five miles south of Loughborough, for centuries and some of their fine eighteenth-century monuments are to be seen in the village church. The present Hall stands away from the village, at the east end, commanding fine views over Charnwood Forest. It was built on a new site, the old hall having been burnt down in 1822, for the fourth Earl of Lanesborough by the architect Sir James Pennethorne, whose only country house this was. It took some twenty years to build and was not completed until 1852. It was occupied by the Lanesboroughs until the late 1970s, after which it lay unoccupied for some time before being purchased by Mr and Mrs Adam Page. Over a four-year period, from 1981 to 1984, they had the house lovingly restored and have beautifully furnished the interior.

The house is of two storeys, cement-rendered, and the entrance front has two projecting wings and

83. *The garden front of Swithland Hall built in the first half of the nineteenth century after the first house was burned down in 1922.*

in the centre a portico of four short columns in pairs. The garden front has a canted bay running the full height of the house.

WHATTON HOUSE

*W*hatton House lies just to the west of the A6, about five miles north-west of Loughborough. Set in its park with fine views eastward over the Soar Valley, it was built about 1802 for Edward Dawson by John Johnson. By the 1860s Lord Crawshaw's family was living there and they have been there ever since, After a series of fires in the 1870s and 1880s, the house was extensively remodelled. During the last war, the house was requisitioned for use as a maternity hospital for mothers leaving the cities because of the bombing and during that time more than 2,000 babies were born there.

The house, built in a classical style, of ashlar with hipped slate roofs, is of three storeys. The

84. *(above) The entrance front to Whatton House with its porch.*

85. *(right) The garden front of Whatton House shows the original five-bay house to the right to which an extension to the left was added in the late nineteenth century.*

the north front a library consisting of one tall storey. In 1974, the conservatory which lay to the south-west of the house was replaced by a colonnade. The interior of the house contains delicate marble fireplaces in an early nineteenth-century style, which are either original or copied after the fires. The stables, of whitewashed brick, mostly of about 1802, are attached to the rear of the house and surround three sides of a courtyard. To the south of the house are formal gardens, created after 1876, including a Chinese Garden with numerous Chinese objects. The park and gardens are included in the English Heritage Register of Parks and Gardens of Special Historic Interest.

original house was five bays long and three bays wide, to which were added in the late nineteenth century bays to the west and north, an eastern projection, and the entrance front including of a porch with Tuscan columns and a pediment, and to

WISTOW HALL

Wistow lies some eight mile south-east of the centre of Leicester. There was a village here which has disappeared and only the Hall and church remain. The Halford family acquired the manor of Wistow in 1603 and probably built the present house at that time, possibly on or near the site of an earlier medieval house. Richard Halford was created a baronet in 1641 for services to the Royalist cause

and, between 1768 and 1780, his descendant, Sir William Halford, modernised the house. Further alterations were made by Sir Henry Halford who succeeded to the property in about 1815 and found it in poor condition. Some other minor alterations were made by the Halfords in the early twentieth century.

The house today retains the form of a large early seventeenth-century building, consisting of two stories with attics. Built of red brick with stone dressings, it is now completely stuccoed on all sides, and with a Swithland slate roof. The principal entrance front, of two-and-a-half storeys, faces east, with a one-storey vestibule between projecting wings which was remodelled about 1815. Inside is an impressive entrance hall, dating from the late eighteenth century, above which can be seen some elements of the seventeenth-century roof. The staircase has a later eighteenth-century wrought-iron balustrade of a simple lyre pattern. Charles I stayed here before the Battle of Naseby and he and Prince Rupert left their saddles here, still preserved in the house, after changing horses on their flight after the battle. Today, the house is owned by Mr Timothy Brooks, Lord Lieutenant of Leicestershire.

86. *The entrance front to Wistow Hall, built in the early eighteenth century and remodelled in about 1815.*

WITHCOTE HALL

Withcote lies due east of Leicester close to the Rutland border. It is yet another example of a village which has disappeared, having been depopulated in early Tudor times for cattle and sheep pastures. Today, only the Hall and church, really its private chapel, stand. Described by Pevsner as "A plain, reasonable, golden-coloured and extremely lovable house", Withcote Hall was built in the early eighteenth century for Matthew Johnson, who was married to the Palmer family, incorporating fragments of an earlier house. Another Palmer, the Reverend Henry, "entirely restored" the house some time in the first half of the nineteenth century, though his work is more evident inside than out. The house is of finely coursed limestone with limestone ashlar dressings, a big coved cornice and Swithland

slate roofs, and comprises two storeys with attics. The west entrance front consists of seven bays, the central three bays projecting slightly and carrying a pediment. In the centre is a porch, probably a nineteenth-century addition with a pediment with a shield of arms. The south garden front is of nine bays with the two bays at each end projecting. the central doorway has a broken pediment carrying an urn. The interior contains two rooms with very richly worked panelled plaster ceilings, specially commissioned by Henry Palmer. The central hall has a late

87. *The south, garden front of Withcote Hall, built in the early eighteenth century and restored a century later.*

eighteenth-century cantilevered stone staircase. By the house is its private chapel, now maintained as a redundant church. Dating originally from 1530 to 1540, it contains some excellent contemporary stained glass and a fine mainly eighteenth century interior with wood panelling and reredos.

RUTLAND

AYSTON HALL

There was a manor house at Ayston, near Uppingham, in the Middle Ages, which was rebuilt in the 1720s. However the present house,

88. Ayston Hall was built in 1807 in a plain classical style. This photograph shows the entrance front, with its porch, to the right, and the garden front to the left.

which incorporates parts of the earlier buildings, dates from 1807 when it was built for Sir George Fludyer by H. D. Legg. The Fludyers first came here in the eighteenth century and lived in the hall until 1924 when the last Lady Fludyer died. The estate then passed to Vere Finch, a member of a branch of the Finch family of Burley-on-the-Hill. The Finches lived in the mansion for over 50 years and it was they who had a substantial part of it demolished in the 1970s. In recent years the house has passed through several hands and the present owners are Mr and Mrs Robinson who have lovingly restored much of it.

The house, of two storeys, is built of ashlar in a plain classical style. The entrance front is of three bays with a porch with two Roman Doric columns and two pilasters supporting a plain entablature. The garden front is of seven bays, with a recessed arch spanning the central three bays. Running round the top of the house is a moulded ashlar cornice and parapet. Alongside the house is a coachhouse which incorporates part of the earlier buildings.

BURLEY-ON-THE-HILL

The mansion stands prominently situated on a hill, some two miles north-east of Oakham, commanding fine views southwards over Rutland Water. The first great house here was built by George Villiers, Duke of Buckingham, formerly of Brooksby in nearby Leicestershire. However, the house suffered at the hands of the Parliamentary forces during the Civil War and fell into a derelict condition.

Daniel Finch, the second Earl of Nottingham and Sixth Earl of Winchelsea, bought the Burley estate in about 1689 and set about building the present great mansion, which was started in 1694 and completed in 1702. The Finch family remained at Burley until 1939 when, upon the death of Wilfred Henry Montgomery Finch, the estate passed to his great-nephew, James Robert Hanbury. In 1989 it

pediments on fluted Ionic pilasters. The centres are flanked on either side by four-bay sections and then two-bay projecting angled pavilions. On either side of the central pediments are balustraded parapets.

The north entrance to the great house is approached through a courtyard flanked by short quadrant Doric colonnades . The house was gutted by fire in 1908 and subsequently restored in its original style. However, the staircase hall, to the east of the entrance hall, survived, with its late seventeenth-century ceiling and wall paintings, as did the dining room of about 1780. The park and gardens, which slope down to the south towards

89. (above) The south front of Burley-on-the -Hill, built between 1694 and 1708 for Daniel Finch, Earl of Nottingham.
90. (right) The north front of Burley-on-the-Hill with its colonnade.

was sold by Joss Hanbury to Asil Nadir, the Turkish Cypriot businessman who had elaborate plans for turning the estate into a leisure complex and golf course. These plans never materialised and, today, the house has been sensitively converted into six separate units by the developer, Kit Martin.

The house itself is of stone, fifteen bays long and seven bays wide. It has a basement and elevated and rusticated ground floor, a first floor of a similar height and a lower second floor. The main north and south facades have centres of three bays with

Rutland Water, are included in the English Heritage Register as being of special historic interest. Within the park are two great formal early eighteenth-century avenues, running south and east of the mansion.

CLIPSHAM HALL

*L*ike many in the two counties, Clipsham Hall, on the northern edge of Rutland, shows evidence of building of different periods. Apart from a stone wall of 1582, the oldest part of the house, which is composed of stone for which Clipsham is famous, is on the north side and dates from about 1700. The major part of the house, two-and-a-half storeys high, dates from the eighteenth century and consists of 10 bays with its main front facing east. According to Pevsner, this was probably the back of the house until about 1881 when J. H. Davenport-Handley, who inherited the estate from his bachelor uncle who had purchased it in 1865, added a new centrepiece of three bays with a pediment and a spectacular Tuscan portico. The west front has a central pedimented bay with an arched doorway. Davenport-Handley also built the neo-Jacobean stables and coach house here at some time in the 1880s. The present owner, Sir David Davenport-Handley, is a direct descendant. Leading to the east front is the famous topiary Yew Avenue clipped to various designs and managed by the Forestry Commission for the owners of the Hall. The nearby quarry was worked for centuries until 1953 when it was found to be exhausted.

91. *The main east front of Clipsham Hall with its spectacular Tuscan portico dates from the sixteenth century.*

EXTON HALL

*T*he Haringtons of Exton, five miles east-north-east of Oakham, a dominant family in sixteenth- and seventeenth-century Rutland, first came here in the mid-fifteenth century. At some stage they presumably built a house at Exton but were forced to sell the manor in the early seventeenth century. The buyer was Sir Baptist Hicks, a rich London merchant who, having no sons, upon his death the manor came to his son-in-law, the first Baron Noel of Ridlington and Master of Game in the then Leighfield Forest. Here, the Noels have remained ever since, becoming first Viscounts Campden and then, from 1682, Earls of Gainsborough.

The Noels first built a house here in the early seventeenth century which was burnt out in 1810. The ruins of the Old Hall still, a scheduled ancient monument, stand, including the walls of the great

92. *The main west front of Exton Hall dating largely from 1811 and added to in the 1850s. To the right is the chapel of 1888-9 built in a thirteenth-century style.*

hall, some 180 metres south of the present Hall. These were further reduced by fire in 1915. Exton Hall today consists of an older timber-framed building to which a new large stone house was added in 1811 by the architect John Linnell Bond. The main west facade includes what Pevsner describes as "three Tudorish gables assorting strangely with three plain Venetian windows and a classical porch". Then, between 1851 and 1853, the architect Henry Roberts made substantial additions to the house, almost quadrupling it in size. The additions, to the northwest and the south of Linnell's house, comprise large Jacobethan blocks with big bay windows, gables and polygonal turrets. To the right of the house, and attached to it, is a chapel built in 1868-9 in a thirteenth-century style. In the grounds of the park is the Church of St Peter and St Paul notable chiefly for its splendid collection of monuments, including those of members of the Harington and Noel families. The parkland, included in the English Heritage Register, which was landscaped in the latter part of the eighteenth century, includes a large lake and various garden buildings including Fort Henry, a late eighteenth-century Gothick summer house.

HAMBLETON HALL

Situated in the village of Hambleton, which stands on a peninsula poking out into the western side of Rutland Water, the Hall was built in 1881 as a hunting box for Walter Marshall, a wealthy brewer. After his death, the house passed through various hands until it was purchased for use as a hotel when, between 1979 and 1980, the interior was transformed. Built in a picturesque 'Old English' style, of coursed and squared rubble with ashlar dressings, it has tile hanging to the first floor. The asymmetrical

93. *The south front of Hambleton Hall, overlooking Rutland Water, built in 1881 in an Old English style.*

north entrance front, of two storeys with attics, has a timber-framed dormer window, jetted over a canted bay window. The south front, overlooking Rutland Water, is also asymmetrical. The interior is elaborately decorated in an eclectic manner with ornate fireplaces and inglenook corners. Nearby is a stable quadrangle built in a 1900 Arts and Crafts style.

HAMBLETON OLD HALL

The Hall here, described as "new erected" in 1611, was purchased by Abel Barker, a wool grazier, in 1634. As his family became more prosperous, so his son Abel built a new house at nearby Lyndon in the 1670s. However, although the latter became the family seat, the Barkers continued to own Hambleton Old Hall until the family died out in 1845. The charming early seventeenth-century house, described by Pevsner as the best of its date in Leicestershire, has been altered several times. Of modest size, it is basically an H-plan two-storey house with gabled wings. The south front, which appears originally to have been the entrance front, has an ashlar-faced centre with a Tuscan Loggia on high plinths. The north front, now the entrance front, also has a loggia of four arches with a balustrade, and a porch on the right flanked by Tuscan columns. The interior contains early seventeenth-century doorways and fireplaces and a wide newel staircase of the later seventeenth century. Enclosing the house to the front is a dry stone wall and two pairs of gate piers. The house now stands right by the south-west corner of Rutland Water.

94. *The spectacular north entrance front of Hambleton Old Hall with its loggia and porch.*

LANGHAM OLD HALL

*L*angham Old Hall, a few miles north of Oakham, is a mansion with a core of 1665 which was extensively added to by the architect H. S. Goodhart-Rendel between 1925 and 1930. He created a U-plan house backing the original range. The latter, of rubble coursed and squared with sandstone dressings, faces south and consists of two storeys with mullioned windows, above which are three full dormers with gables and finials. The back of this house, now the entrance front, was greatly enlarged by Goodhart-Rendel in a neo-seventeenth century style Built also of ironstone rubble with sandstone dressings, it is one-and-a-half storeys high with gables springing from the level of the eaves. The door beneath the central gable has Ionic columns and a segmental open pediment containing arms. Finally, Goodhart-Rendel enlarged an irregularly curved stable wing with a gate arch providing the entrance way to the house and with a wooden spire.

95. *The south front of Langham Old Hall dates from 1665.*

LYNDON HALL

*L*yndon Hall, near Manton, lies just south of Rutland Water. The Barker family purchased the manor of Lyndon in 1662 and Abel Barker built a house here between 1671 and 1677. Barker drew up the design of the house himself and supervised its building, a process which is unusually well documented. Abel was made a baronet by Charles II in 1665 and his son, Sir Thomas Barker, twice Sheriff of Rutland, died childless in 1707, when the title passed to another branch of the family, the Barkers of South Luffenham. In 1835, the last Barker, Samuel, died without sons and the estate passed to his daughters from whom it was purchased by their cousin, the Reverend Edward Brown. Upon his death, he was succeeded as owner of the estate by his nephew Edward Conant, and the Conants have lived at Lyndon ever since.

A charmingly modest stone house, of what Pevsner calls square solidity, each of the four fronts consists of seven bays and two storeys with a hipped roof and three dormer windows. At the corners of the house are rusticated quoins. Each front has a doorway with a swan-necked pediment on pilasters,

96. The east front of the attractive Lyndon Hall built in the 1670s.

to which on the north front a nineteenth-century porch was added. The main entrance was originally on the south front which leads into the park, but this was moved to the north front, also in the nineteenth century. The interior contains some good nineteenth-century plasterwork and fittings.

Source: John Cornforth, "Lyndon Hall, Rutland, The Home of Lady Conant", *Country Life*, 140, 1966, . pp.1212-15.

NORTH LUFFENHAM HALL

*T*he village of North Luffenham lies just off the south-east corner of Rutland Water. Originally the manor house, the mansion here became the Hall when an earlier adjoining Hall was demolished in 1801. It was owned by the Harington family from 1538 to 1599 and then by the Digbys until the

97. The north entrance front to North Luffenham Hall is of two dates. The range to the left, dates from the mid-eighteenth century while that to the right, with its elaborate Dutch gable, dates from the early seventeenth century.

mid-eighteenth century. The north entrance front is in two main sections. That to the left, dating from the mid to the late eighteenth century, is of two storeys with a central projecting three-storey gable. The section to the right is an early seventeenth-century range of two-and-a-half storeys with a large elaborate Dutch gable and a doorway surmounted by a stone coat of arms of the Digby family. The south front had added to it an early eighteenth-century classical facade of four bays, with a cornice above and hipped dormers. Later, a doorway was added with a stone canopy, leading up to which are seven stone steps. To the left is a two-storey service wing built between 1910 and 1911. Inside is an early seventeenth-century oak staircase with turned balusters and early eighteenth-century panelling in the Drawing and Dining rooms.

98. *The south front of North Luffenham Hall shows the classical facade added to it in the early eighteenth century and to the left the early twentieth-century service wing.*

SOUTH LUFFENHAM HALL

*T*he village lies a mile south of North Luffenham and the hall is on its eastern edge alongside the A6121. A delightful small, symmetrical house, typical of the late seventeenth century, it is built of ashlar and coarse stone, with rusticated quoins and a Collyweston slate roof. Of two-and-a-half storeys and a basement, it is five bays wide on each side and has a central doorway on the garden front with steps leading up to it. The hipped slate roof has two dormer windows on each side. Nearby is an early eighteenth-century stable block.

99. *The garden front of South Luffenham Hall, a delightful late seventeenth-century stone house.*

TOLETHORPE HALL

Tolethorpe Hall lies near Little Casterton, on the east side of Rutland. A house has existed here since the Middle Ages and Robert Browne, described as "the father of religious non-conformism" was born here in about 1550. The Hall was rebuilt by the Browne family either in the late sixteenth or early seventeenth century. It was enlarged soon after and altered again in the middle of the eighteenth century when it belonged to Thomas Trollope. It eventually came to Charles Ormiston who made further alterations in about 1867. Today, it is the home of the Stamford Shakespeare Players.

The house, built on an H-plan, shows features of the different periods of its building and remodelling. The north front, of two storeys with attics, dates from the late sixteenth or early seventeenth century and is typical of the period with its mullioned windows, its slightly projecting gabled wings and its asymmetrically placed gabled porch. It consists of six bays, four in the centre, and one on each side projecting with a gable. Adjacent to the west gable is an altered seventeenth-century porch with a gable and a semi-circular entrance arch. The facade was partly refaced with mid-eighteenth century ashlar. The south front, which has also been altered at various times, has two large projecting cross-gabled wings.

100. *The north front of Tolethorpe Hall dates from the late sixteenth century or earlier.*

Glossary of Architectural Terms

architrave a lintel, the lowest part of the **entablature**. Also used to describe the moulded frame of a door or window.

Arts and Crafts Movement A late nineteenth-century movement which began in England promoting craftsmanship and particularly associated with William Morris.

ashlar masonry made up of large blocks laid in regular courses with even faces and fine joints.

baldachino or **ciborium** a canopy over an altar or tomb, usually supported by columns.

balusters small posts or pillars, usually circular in section, with a curving outline.

balustrade a railing or coping supported by short pillars or columns.

Baroque a term usually applied to the architecture current in Italy in the seventeenth century, combining architecture, sculpture and painting to achieve a substantial impact on the spectator. English Baroque was less well defined and developed in the late seventeenth century with the work of Sir Christopher Wren and later with Nicholas Hawksmoor and Sir John Vanbrugh.

bays external divisions of the elevations of buildings marked by windows, columns, arches, etc.

brackets small stone projections supporting horizontal members.

bull's eye window a round or oval window set horizontally, usually with glazing bars.

buttress a support, of brick or stone, built against a wall to give it stability.

capital the uppermost part of a column or pilaster. Each of the Greek orders of architecture had a capital of different form.

ciborium see **baldachino**

coffer an ornamental panel sunk into a ceiling.

colonnade a row of columns supporting an **entablature**.

Corinthian see **orders of architecture**

corbels projecting blocks of stone, brick or wood supporting weights.

cornice the ornamental moulding that runs around the walls of a room, linking them to the ceiling. The term is also used to describe a moulded ledge, projecting along the top of a building or feature.

crockets carved projections, usually in leaf form, decorating gables, spires and pinnacles.

cruck trusses pairs of curved timbers which form the main framework of early timber-framed buildings and support the roof.

diaper an overall surface pattern of lozenges or squares on brickwork, achieved by using bricks of two colours.

Doric see **orders of architecture**.

dormer window a vertical window standing out from a sloping roof and having a roof of its own.

entablature the upper part of the classical orders of architecture, comprising the architrave, frieze and cornice.

gables the upper parts of walls, often triangular, at the end of a pitched roof.

garderobe a medieval privy.

Gothic Revival a revival of Gothic architecture in England from the mid-eighteenth to the mid-nineteenth century. Associated, about 1755, in a playful form with Horace Walpole's villa at Strawberry Hill, near Twickenham, it assumed a more serious form in the early nineteen century.

Gothick the fanciful early phase of the **Gothic Revival**.

Greek Revival in the mid-eighteenth century, Greek architecture became better known and from about the 1760s some architects attempted to design buildings conforming closely to Greek models. The style continued in England until about 1840.

hipped roof a roof with sides sloping back towards the ridge.

Ionic see **orders of architecture**.

Jacobethan a mixture of Elizabethan and Jacobean styles used in the later nineteenth century.

jetty the projecting upper storey of a timber-framed building.

keystone the central wedge-shaped block of an arch.

loggia a covered gallery along one side of a building, open to the air.

mullions vertical stone or wooden divisions splitting windows into compartments or 'lights'.

Neo-classical the style of architecture, based on Greek and Roman examples, which dominated English architecture from about 1760 to 1790.

newel a spiral staircase.

ogee arch a pointed arch made up of two convex arcs above and two concave arcs below.

orders of architecture a system used to categorise various types of classical architecture based on different types of columns. the simplest is the **Doric** order with its fluted columns and plain slab on top. The **Ionic** order has a slenderer fluted column with spiral scrolls on the front and back of the capital. The **Corinthian** order has a fluted column with a capital representing an acanthus growing in a basket. All these orders are Greek and the Romans introduced a **Tuscan** order, a simplified Doric with unfluted columns.

oriel window a bay window projecting from an upper storey, usually supported on **corbels.**

Palladianism an architectural movement flourishing in England between about 1720 and 1750, following the examples and principles of the sixteenth-century Venetian architect, Andrea Palladio.

Palladianism freely adapted Imperial Roman architecture.

pediment a low-pitched gable over a door, window or portico, originally triangulated but sometimes segmental.

Picturesque a late eighteenth-century principle mainly concerned with arranging architectural elements as parts of their landscape setting in a pleasingly irregular fashion.

pilaster a rectangular column projecting slightly from a wall, usually with a decorative rather than a structural purpose.

porch a covered entrance to a building.

porte-cochere a porch large enough to allow a vehicle through a building or to allow passengers to alight before entering a building.

portico a porch enclosed by a row of columns and open on at least one side.

quoins dressed stones forming the corner of a wall.

rainwater heads a metal container, often decorated, at the top of a rainwater pipe, to collect the outflow from a roof gutter.

rendering a waterproof coating, usually plaster or cement, applied to an external wall.

rubble masonry made with rough uncut stones.

rustication masonry made up of blocks or courses of stone with deeply-recessed joints, often with a roughened surface.

transoms the horizontal members between the lights in windows.

Tudor English architecture spanning the period from the accession of Henry VII in 1485 to the death of Elizabeth I in 1603, but often restricted to the first half of the sixteenth century.

Tuscan see **orders of architecture**.

vermiculation a form of rustication in which the masonry is ornamented with stylised grooves like worm-casts.

For this glossary, I have drawn upon three major sources: John Harris and Jill Lever, *Illustrated Glossary of Architecture, 850-1830*, Faber and Faber, 1966; Nikolaus Pevsner et al., *The Buildings of England, Leicestershire and Rutland*, Penguin, Second Edition, 1984, "Glossary", pp.525-557; and Edward Luce Smith, *Dictionary of Art Terms*, Thames and Hudson, 1995. For further reference, these books are recommended.

Visiting and Looking at Our Country Houses

As the great majority of historic country houses in Leicestershire and Rutland are in private hands and as few of their owners open them to the public, only three of them are regularly and frequently open. Two of them, Belvoir Castle and Stanford Hall are at opposite ends of the county of Leicestershire. *Belvoir Castle*, in the north-east corner of the county, is open most days of the week from April to October, while *Stanford Hall*, down on the Northamptonshire border, is open mainly at weekends, from Easter through to the end of September. *Belgrave Hall*, the third, now run as a museum by the City of Leicester, and with fine gardens, is open most days, entrance being free. The two late medieval castles in Leicestershire, the predecessors of the 'true' country house are both in the care of English Heritage. *Ashby-de-la-Zouch Castle* is open daily from the beginning of April to the end of September, and, at the time of writing, *Kirby Muxloe Castle* is open at some weekends.

A number of other fine houses are open to the public on occasion, as the venues of craft fairs and similar events. These include the houses at *Beaumanor, Brooksby, Nevill Holt* and *Prestwold*. Visitors to the permanent craft studios in the former stables at *Staunton Harold* can also see the exterior of the house as can those attending Shakespearean productions at *Tolethorpe Hall*. Some of our historic houses have also been turned into hotels, including those at *Market Bosworth, Rothley, Stapleford* and *Hambleton*.

Visitors to *Bradgate Park* can inspect at close quarters the ruins of the great house.

Finally, some houses may be seen, discreetly, from nearby public roads: these include *Baggrave Hall, Ingarsby Old Hall, Launde Abbey*, and *Scraptoft Hall*. And *Braunstone Hall* is in a public park in Leicester.

Bibliography

Bennett: J. D. Bennett, *The Vanished Houses of Leicestershire*, Leicester Museums, 1971.

Broughton: Heather E.Broughton, *Family and Estate Records in the Leicestershire Record Office*, Leicestershire Museums, Arts and Records Service, 1991.

Cantor and Squires: Leonard Cantor and Anthony Squires, *The Historic Parks and Gardens of Leicestershire and Rutland*, Kairos Press, 1997.

Counds: David Counds, "A Celebration of Historic Houses", *NADFAS News*, Autumn/Winter 1988, pp.13-15.

Harris and Lever: John Harris and Jill Lever, *The Illustrated Glossary of Architecture, 850-1830*, Faber and Faber, 1966.

Hoskins (1949): W. G. Hoskins, *Midland England*, Batsford, 1949.

Hoskins (1950): W. G. Hoskins, *The Heritage of Leicestershire*, City of Leicester, 1950.

Hoskins (1957): W. G. Hoskins, *Leicestershire* Hodder and Stoughton, 1957.

Littlejohn: David Littlejohn, *The Fate of the English Country House*, Oxford University Press, 1997.

Oakley: Glynis Oakley, *A History of Gopsall*, Barncraft Printing, 1996.

Pevsner: Nicolaus Pevsner, *The Buildings of England: Leicestershire and Rutland*, Second Edition, Revised by Elizabeth Williamson with Geoffrey K. Brandwood, Penguin, 1984.

Squires: Anthony Squires, *Donington Park and the Hastings Connection*, Kairos Press, 1996.

Stevenson and Squires: Joan Stevenson and Anthony Squires, *Bradgate Park, Childhood Home of Lady Jane Grey*, Kairos Press, 1994.

Waites: Bryan Waites (Ed.), *A Celebration of Rutland*, Multum in Parvo Press, 1994.

Wessell: Caroline Wessell, *Lost Mansions around Desford and Leicester Forest West*, Desford & District Local History Group, 1986.

Zientek: Jan Zientek, "Great Houses of Leicestershire", *Village Voice, The Magazine for Leicestershire and Rutland*, Autumn 1986, p.18.

References

1. Littlejohn, pp.309-311.
2. Ibid. p.311.
3. Hoskins (1950), p.58.
4. Cantor and Squires, p.45.
5. Stevenson and Squires, pp.30-1.
6. Hoskins (1949), p.52.
7. Broughton, p.2.
8. Hoskins (1950), p.63.
9. Pevsner, p.249.
10. Ibid., p.357.
11. Hoskins (1950) p.66.
12. Littlejohn, p.28.
13. Pevsner, p.164.
14. Oakley, p.36.
15. Pevsner, p.489.
16. Hoskins (1950), p.68.
17. Bennett.
18. Pevsner, p.426.
19. Harris and Lever, pp.47-8.
20. Pevsner, p.349.
21. Ibid., p.398.
22. Bennett.
23. Zientek, p.18.
24. Littlejohn, p.49.
25. Counds, p.13.
26. Littlejohn, p.55

Index

A
Appleby Magna: 7
Ashby Folville Manor: **19**, 26, **32**
Ashby, George: 17, 58
Ashby, Shuckburgh: 59
Ashby-de-la-Zouch Castle: 7, **8**, 14, 82
Ayre, John: 43
Ayston Hall: **19**, 25, **73**

B
Babington family: 12, 16, 61
Baggrave Hall: 22, 32-**33**, 82
Bagworth: 8
Bainbrigge: 50
Bale, Sir John: 17, 39
Bannister, Sir Robert: 46, 47
Barkby Hall: 16, 24, 30, **34**
Barker family: 18, 76, 78
Beatty, Admiral: 38
Beaumanor Park: **19**, **25**, 27, **34**-35, 82
Beaumont family: 24, 40, 44
Belgrave Hall: 19, **20**, **35**, 37, 82
Belville, Frank: 26
Belvoir Castle: 12, **15**, 23, **25**, 30, **36**-37, 82
Berners family: 47
Billery: 57
Birstall Hall: 28
Bishop, Sir Michael: 42
Blow: 57
Bodley: 59
Bond, John Linnell: 76
Bonomi, Joseph: 45
Bowlker, Rev C. A.: 53
Bradgate House: **10**, 11, 26, 27
Bradgate Park: 10, 26, 28, 82
Brassey, Captain Harold: 51
Braunstone Hall: 22, **37**, 82
Braye, Lady: 64
Brooks, Timothy: 71
Brooksby Hall: 15, 37-**38**, 73, 82
Brown, Capability: 66
Brown, Rev. Edward: 78
Browne, Robert: 80
Buckingham, Duke of: 38, 73
Buckminster Park: **23**, 27
Burleigh Hall: 24, 27, **29**
Burley-on-the-Hill: **15**, 18, 30, 73-**74**
Burn, William: 58
Burnaby family: 32

C
Campden, Viscounts: 7**5**
Carlton Curlieu Hall: 13, 17, **39**
Cave family: 12, 18, 30, 32, 46, 47, 64
Cavendish House: **12**, 13
Cavendish, William: 13
Cheney, Colonel: 43
Cheshire, Leonard: 67

Clark family: 48
Clipsham Hall: 13, 15, 74-**75**
Coaker, Charles: 50
Cockaigne, Sir William: 13
Cockerell, F. P.: 40
Cold Overton Hall: 15, 17, 39-**40**
Coleorton Hall: 24, 40-**41**
Conant, Edward: 78
Conley, Rosemary: 60
Constable Maxwell family: 45
Cotes Hall: 13, 16, **28**
Cottesmore Hall: 29, 30
Cradock, Edmund: 19, 35
Cradock, Joseph: 22
Crawshaw, Lord: 69
Cromwell, Gregory: 49
Cromwell, Thomas: 12
Cunard, Edward: 53
Cunard, Sir Bache: 53, 54
Curzon, Nathaniel: 50

D
Dance, George: 40
Danets Hall: 27, **28**
Danvers family: 69
Davenport-Handley, J. H.: 75
Dawson, Edward: 24, 48, 69
Devonshire, Duke of: 17, 28
Devonshire, Earl of: 13
Digby family: 78, 79
Dixie family: 18, 52
Donington Hall: **19**, **23**, **25**, 27, 30, 41-4**2**
Donington-le-Heath: 7
Dorset, Marquis of: 10

E
Edmondthorpe Hall: 13, 16, 27, **28**
Edwyn, John: 22, 32
Ellis, John: 35
Elmesthorpe: 13
Exton Hall: 30, **75**-76
Exton Old Hall: 13, **17**, 28

F
Farnham family: 60
Ferrers, Earl: 67
Fielding, William: 17
Finch family: 18, 48, 73
Fludyer family: 73
Fontaine, Sir Erasmus: 13
Fortescue family: 45
Fortescue Turville, Francis: 46
Fowke, Thomas: 51

G
Gaddesby Hall: **43**
Gainsborough, Earls of: 75
Garendon Hall: **20**, 25, 27
Garendon Park: **21**, 29
Gemmill family: 56
Gillies Shields, John: 42
Goadby Marwood Hall: **44**

Gopsall Hall: **21**, 26, 27, 29
Gotch, J. A: 59
Grace Dieu Manor: 12, 25, 34, 44-**45**
Gretton, Frederick: 42
Gretton, John: 65
Grey family: 10, 25
Gumley Hall: **22**, 27, 29

H
Halford family: 16, 22, 48, 70
Hambleton Hall: **76**, 82
Hambleton Old Hall: 76-**77**
Hanbury, James Robert: 73
Harborough, Earl of: 65
Harington family: 75, 78
Hastings family: 36, 41, 42
Hastings, William: 7, 9, 10
Hazlerigg family: 19, 30, 54, 55
Heathcote, Sir Gilbert: 21
Herrick family: 25, 34
Hesilrige family: 19, 54
Hewett, George: 18
Hicks, Sir Baptist: 75
Historic Houses Association: 27
Howe, Earl: 21
Humberstone Hall: 27, 28
Huntingdon, Earl of: 12
Husbands Bosworth Hall: 13, 45-**46**

I
Ingarsby Old Hall: **46**-47, 82

J
Jackson, James Alexander: 26
Jekyll, Gertrude: 26, 29, 51
Jennens, Charles: 21, 26
Johnson, John: 69
Johnson, Matthew: 19

K
Keythorpe Hall: **47**
Kirby Bellars Hall: **13**
Kirby Muxloe Castle: 7, 8, **9**, 14, 82

L
Lanesborough, Earls of: 24, 69
Langham Old Hall: **77**
Langton Hall: 15, 47-**48**
Launde Abbey: 12, 15, **18**, 30, 48-**49**, 82
Legg, H. D: 73
Leicester Abbey: 12
de Lisle, the Squire: 59
de Lisle, Ambrose Phillipps: 21, 25, 34, 44
Lockington Hall: 18, **50**
Lowesby Hall: 19, **51**
Lutyens, Sir Edwin: 26, 29, 38, 51
Lyndon Hall: **18**, **78**

M
Manners family: 12, 24, 30, 36
Market Bosworth Hall: **14**, **18**, 30, **52**, 82

Marshall, Walter: 76
Martin, Kit: 74
Martinsthorpe Hall: 13, **17**, 28
Meynell, Hugo: 47, 59

N
Nadir, Asil: 33, 74
Nash, John: 22
Nevill Holt Hall: 11, **53**-54, 82
Nevill, William: 53
Noel family: 12, 13, 17, 30, 75
Nollekens, Joseph: 37
Normanton Hall: 21, 27, **29**
North Luffenham Hall: 78-**79**
Noseley Hall: 14, 19, 30, 54-**55**

O
Ogden, C. E.: 43
Ord, Rev. James: 48
Ormiston, Charles: 80
Osbaston Hall: 19, **55-56**
Otway-Cave, Sarah: 64

P
Packe family: 57, 58
Packe-Drury-Lowe family: 30, 58
Page, Mr and Mrs Adam: 69
Paget family: 27
Palladio, Andrea: 21
Palmer, Henry: 72
Palmer, Sir Geoffrey: 39
Palmer, Thomas: 11, 53, 54
Papillon Hall: **19**, 26, 27, **29**
Payton, John: 65
Peatling Parva Hall: **56**-57
Pennethorne, Sir James: 69
Phillipps family: 20, 44
Pochin family: 16, 24, 30, 34
Powys-Keck family: 26
Prestwold Hall: 24, 30, 82, **57**-58
Pugin, A. W: 44, 45

Q
Quenby Hall: 13, 14, 17, **18**, **58**-59
Quorn Hall: 18, **59**-60
Quorn House: **19**, **24**, **60**

R
Ragdale Hall: 13, 27
Ragdale Old Hall: **16**, 29
Railton, William: 25, 34, 44, 49
Rawlins Coleman, Cecil: 48
Repton, Humphry: 22, 23, 24, 42
Rimmington, Mr and Mrs: 32
Roberts, Henry: 76
Roninson, Mr and Mrs: 73
Rothley Hall: 12, 13, 16, **61**, 82
Ruding family: 27
Rutland, Dukes of: 12, 23, 36

S
Saxon, Samuel: 23
Scott, Charles Tollemache: 52
Scraptoft Hall: 19, 30, **62**, 82
Shenton Hall: 13, 17, **63**
Sherard, Bennet: 18

Sherard, Thomas: 11, 65
Shirley family: 16, 22, 67
Simpson, John: 48
Skeffington family: 63
Skeffington Hall: 24, **63**-64
Skipwith family: 16, 28, 58
Smith, Francis: 44, 65
Smith, Roger: 16
Smith, Sir William: 48, 64, 65
South Luffenham Hall: **79**
St John, John: 17, 39
Stamford, Earls of: 11, 26, 28
Stanford Hall: 12, **18**, 30, 32, **64**-65, 82
Stapleford Hall: 30, 42, 82
Stapleford Park: **11**, 18, 65-**66**
Staunton Harold Hall: **14**, **18**, 22, 30, **67**-68, 82
Staveley, Thomas: 47
Storey, Rev. Philip: 50
Stoughton Grange: 26, 27, 29
Stretton Hall: 18, **68**
Swithland Hall: 24, **69**

T
Tailby, William: 64
Talbot family: 35
Thoroton, Rev. Sir John: 36
Thurnby Court: 26, 29
Tickencote Hall: 20, 27, **28**
Todeni, Robert de: 36
Tolethorpe Hall: **80**, 82
Trollope, Thomas: 80
Turville family: 45

V
Vanburgh, Sir John: 20, 28
Vann family: 35
Verney, Margaret: 64
Villiers, George: 38, 73

W
Wagstaff, John: 46
Warner, Edward: 60
Westcotes Hall: 27, 28
Westley, Alderman John: 21
Whatton House: 24, 69-**70**
Wigley family: 19, 62
Wilkins, William: 33, 41, 58
Wilson, Mr and Mrs David: 51
Wilson, Mrs Barbara: 40
Wingfield family: 20, 28
Winstanley family: 22, 37
Wistow Hall: 13, 16, 22, 70-**71**
Withcote Hall: **18**, **19**, 71-**72**
Wollaston family: 17, 19, 51, 63
Wolstan, A. A. D.: 52
Wordsworth, William and Dorothy: 41
Wright, Sir Nathan: 38
Wyatt, James: 36
Wyatt, Matthew Cotes: 37